Backroad Bicycling
in Vermont

Backroad Bicycling in Vermont

TEXT AND PHOTOGRAPHS
BY JOHN S. FREIDIN

With a Foreword by Bill McKibben

THE COUNTRYMAN PRESS
WOODSTOCK, VERMONT

An Invitation to the Reader
Although it is unlikely that the roads you cycle on in these tours will change much
with time, some road signs, landmarks, and other terms may. If you find that
changes have occurred on these routes, please let us know so we may correct them in
future editions. Address all correspondence to:

Editor, Bicycling Guides
The Countryman Press
P.O. Box 748
Woodstock, VT 05091

Library of Congress Cataloging-in-Publication Data
Data has been applied for.

ISBN-13 978-0-88150-692-1
ISBN-10 0-88150-692-3

Published by The Countryman Press, P.O. Box 748, Woodstock, VT 05091

Distributed by W. W. Norton & Company, Inc., 500 Fifth Avenue, New York, NY
10110

Text and cover design by Bodenweber Design
Composition by Faith Hague
Cover photograph of the Champlain Valley just south of St. Albans © Dennis Coello
Maps by Tony Moore © The Countryman Press
Interior photographs by the author unless otherwise specified

Printed in the United States of America

10 9 8 7 6 5 4 3 2 1

For Gail, Abe, and Luke

ACKNOWLEDGMENTS FOR THE FOURTH EDITION Thanks
first to all the men and women who worked with me at Vermont Bicycle
Touring (VBT) and rode on our tours. Without them I never would have
had the knowledge or the opportunity to write this book.

Many cyclists—whom I have met while they were riding these tours,
who have written to me, and whose views I solicited while doing the research for this edition—gave me valuable suggestions. Their enthusi-
asm has spurred me on; their knowledge has made this a better book.

Special thanks go to Neil Quinn and Betsy Bates, who helped design
the Putney-Dummerston tour, and to Steve Lotspeich, Waterbury town
planner, who helped with the Waterbury–Stowe tour. Tyrone Shaw sug-
gested splendid back roads, which I used in the Jeffersonville-Sheldon
tour. Tyrone also gave me the great CD *Maalox, Mylanta, and You,* by
his band, the Oleo Romeos. I regularly listened to it while driving between tours. Beth Karnes, who played a major role in the reconstruc-
tion of the steeple on the Brandon Baptist Church, provided a full story
of that effort. Edith Celley, who led tours for VBT, helped with historical information about her hometown, Haverhill, New Hampshire.
Joseph A. Citro's book, *Green Mountain Ghosts, Ghouls & Unsolved
Mysteries* (Houghton Mifflin, 1994), was helpful for the discussion of
Shard Villa Residental Care Home's ghostly activity in the East
Middlebury– Salisbury tour.

Patrick Clark at Henry Holt and Company was wonderfully helpful
in enabling me to receive permission to quote several lines from Robert
Frost's poem "Birches." David Deen helped me describe the ecological
importance of riparian buffers. Loreen DeGeus of the Vermont
Department of Agriculture cheerfully answered my questions about
dairy farming. Michael Chernick, Esq., of the Vermont Legislative

Council reviewed current Vermont bicycling law for me. The kind hospitality and superb cooking of the owners of two bed & breakfasts—Margaret Ryan of The Albro Nichols House in St. Johnsbury and Sue and Rod Holmes of The Kimball House in Hardwick—made my overnights in the Northeast Kingdom a joy. I heartily recommend them both. Finally, my good friend Bill Goldstein accompanied me on many rides; his companionship and judgment are the best.

The earlier work of others was also invaluable. Most of what I learned of the history of New Haven, my hometown, came from Harold Farnsworth and Robert Rogers's *History of New Haven* (1984). It also increased my understanding of the elaborate connections among the land speculation of Ethan Allen, land grants made by colonial New Hampshire governor Benning Wentworth, and Vermont's decision not to join the Union in 1777.

Two books, which I used often, will also provide bicyclists doing these tours with much valuable information. Christina Tree and Diane E. Foulds's *Vermont: An Explorer's Guide* (Countryman Press, 2006) succinctly describes hundreds of places to stay, eat, and visit. In *Vermont* (Fodor Compass American Guide, 2001), Don Mitchell beautifully reveals the true nature of this special state. *Vermont* is splendidly illustrated with superb photographs by Luke Powell.

For mapping I relied on two books: *Vermont Atlas and Gazetteer* (DeLorme, 2003) and *Vermont Road Atlas* (Jimapco, 2001). Their detailed maps enabled me to identify many back roads that only 10 years ago were nearly invisible.

Jennifer Thompson, my editor at The Countryman Press, tolerated my suggestions as if she wanted to hear them, was always available to answer questions, and made many valuable suggestions. Thanks, Jennifer.

Nature made Vermont a bicyclist's Shangri-La, but human beings must keep it that way. In Vermont, three nonprofit organizations do most of that work. They deserve the support of everyone concerned about a healthy recreational environment. These organizations improve and expand bicycling opportunities, educate cyclists and motorists, and publish valuable guides. They can also help you find a local cycling club or get involved in regional advocacy.

Vermont Bicycle and Pedestrian Coalition (P.O. Box 1234, Montpelier, VT 05601; 802-225-8904; www.vtbikeped.org) promotes safe access to bicycling and walking opportunities statewide. For the sake of our health, economy, environment, and community, the Vermont Bicycle and Pedestrian Coalition advocates for improved laws and funding at both state and local levels and serves as a networking organization for bicycle and walking clubs.

In northwestern Vermont, Local Motion (1 Steele Street #103, Burlington, VT 05401; 802-652-BIKE; www.localmotion.org) promotes bicycling, walking, running, in-line skating, and the facilities that make such travel safe, easy, and fun. It serves as a clearinghouse for cycling maps and books on New England, Québec, and New York. Phone orders are welcome. Its Trailside Center on the Burlington Bike Path provides bike and blade rentals as well as maps.

Lake Champlain Bikeways is a 1,100-mile network of on- and off-road bikeways throughout the Champlain valley of Vermont, New York, and Québec. Maps and cue sheets are available online at www.champlain bikeways.org.

Most of all, I want to thank Gail, Abe, and Luke for their daily support of my efforts to make this the best bicycle touring guide ever. Gail consistently enabled me to have the time to do research and to write. Abe and Luke offered excellent suggestions, and their presence always made working at home a delight for me.

New Haven, Vermont
October 2005

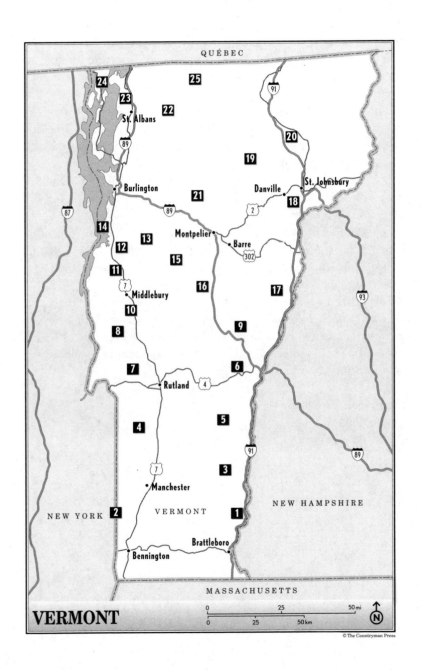

VERMONT

QUÉBEC

NEW YORK

VERMONT

NEW HAMPSHIRE

MASSACHUSETTS

St. Albans
Burlington
Montpelier • Barre
Danville
St. Johnsbury
Middlebury
Rutland
Manchester
Bennington
Brattleboro

© The Countryman Press

0   25   50 mi
0   25   50 km

CONTENTS

IV. NORTHWESTERN VERMONT

PREFACE John Freidin has written a book for people who want to see my native Vermont without hurry, and to experience it with all their senses. His knowledge and love of our beckoning state shine through his descriptions of its people and its rich history, as well as its nooks and vales and mountain greenery. And his clear instructions will guide you confidently to your own backroad adventures.

Backroad Bicycling in Vermont is a guide for travelers who want to get off the beaten path. John has chosen those less-traveled roads that make all the difference to the Vermont you will see while you are here, and that you will remember long afterward.

So if you really want to see and breathe Vermont—heed John's advice. Use this book and take your time. You will discover why those of us who have lived here all our lives would never live anywhere else.

—U.S. Senator Patrick Leahy

BACKROAD BICYCLE TOURS AT A GLANCE

RIDE	TERRAIN	DISTANCE IN MILES (UNPAVED PORTION)
1. Putney–Dummerston	Easy to moderate Moderate to difficult	38.6 (5.9) 44 (9.3)
2. Arlington–North Bennington	Moderate	50.1 (11.1)
3. Chester–Grafton	Easy to moderate side trip	26.8 (4.6) plus 3-mile
4. Middletown Springs–Pawlet	Moderate to difficult	28.3 plus 2.4-mile side trip
5. Proctorsville–Felchville	Moderate	27.2 (3.2)
6. Woodstock–Quechee	Moderate to difficult	25.3 (2.2)
7. Brandon–West Rutland	Easy to moderate	36 (1.4)
8. Brandon–Fort Ticonderoga	Easy to moderate Moderate Moderate to difficult	15.9 (3.2) 32.7 (1.9) 45.8 (1.9)
9. South Royalton–Strafford	Difficult	27.7
10. East Middlebury–Salisbury	Easy	25 (4.6)
11. Vergennes–Middlebury	Easy to moderate	25.2
12. New Haven–Vergennes	Easy	30 (3.5)

GOOD FOR YOUNGER RIDERS?	HIGHLIGHTS
	Good for fat-tired bicycling and riders of differing abilities; superb water scenes; farmland; orchards; magnificent woods
	Two covered bridges; good for fat-tired bicycles; swimming; Norman Rockwell exhibit; Park-McCullough mansion; fine views
	Four covered bridges; antiques; 19th-century architecture; local fine art; exquisite village of Grafton; cheese factory; swimming; good for fat-tired bicycles
	Bucolic; alternately challenging, exhilarating, and blissful glorious in autumn; ice cream at restored railroad station; swimming; very quiet
	Shaded climb leads to 6-mile exhilarating descent; rivers; spectacular in fall; streams; swimming; trout fishing; stone houses; good for fat-tired bicycles
	Covered bridges; elegant Woodstock village; rivers; horse farms; arts, crafts, antiques; Billings Farm and Museum; Marsh-Billings-Rockefeller park
	White-marble town of Proctor; Wilson Castle; Vermont Marble Exhibit; fine food, architecture, and crafts in Brandon; sweeping Green Mountains views
	Perfect for riders of differing abilities; panoramic mountain views; fine food and architecture; crafts, antiques; Revolutionary history; dairy farms
	Three covered bridges; superb architecture; Justin Morrill home; Vermont Law School; stunning 18th-century meetinghouse
Yes	Swimming, hiking; lakeshore riding; 6 miles from Middlebury restaurants, craft galleries, and museums
	Two-lane covered bridge; Morgan Horse Farm; dairy farms; theater; good food; arts, crafts; museums; Middlebury College; panoramic views
Yes	Fabulous views; good food; fine architecture; walking guide to Vergennes; quiet roads; dairy farms

BACKROAD BICYCLE TOURS AT A GLANCE

RIDE	TERRAIN	DISTANCE IN MILES (UNPAVED PORTION)
13. Bristol–Hinesburg	Moderate to difficult	36.7
14. North Ferrisburgh– Essex, New York	Easy to moderate	31 (4.2) or 26.5 (4.2) plus 5-mile side trip
15. Waitsfield–Warren	Moderate to difficult	19 (0.3)
16. Randolph–Brookfield	Moderate Moderate to difficult	42 (2.7) 26 (2.7)
17. Fairlee–Haverhill, New Hampshire	Easy to moderate	24.1 or 16.2
18. Barnet–St. Johnsbury	Moderate to difficult	50.8 (7.4) or 35.6 (2.7)
19. Hardwick– Craftsbury Common	Moderate to difficult Moderate	34.1 27 (0.9); plus 6.4-mile Fat-Tire Challenge
20. Lyndonville–Barton	Easy to moderate	49.7
21. Waterbury–Stowe	Moderate to difficult	31.2 (15.1)
22. Jefferson–Sheldon	Moderate	49.7 (1.8), 40.1 (3.8), or 34.8
23. St. Albans–Swanton	Easy	28.7 plus side trips of 2.2 and 6 miles
24. Alburg–Isle La Motte	Easy	34.7 (1.4) or 22.8 (1.4)
25. Montgomery–Richford	Moderate to difficult	22.6 or 33.7

GOOD FOR YOUNGER RIDERS?	HIGHLIGHTS
	Good restaurants; mountain views; waterfall and river swimming; band concerts; Bristol creemee stand
Yes	Covered bridge; ferry rides across Lake Champlain; swimming; historic village; two ice cream shops; Shelburne Museum
	Two covered bridges; panoramic views; swimming; soaring in a glider; arts, crafts, antiques; summer theater; music; golf; polo; good eating
	Brookfield floating bridge; swimming; Chandler Music Hall and Gallery; Norwich University; Porter Music Box Museum; farms; quiet roads
Yes	Lake and river coastline; beautiful villages of Haverhill and Orford; hot-air balloon rides; architectural scavenger hunt; antiques
	Handsome village of Peacham; St. Johnsbury Athenaeum, Fairbanks Museum of Natural History; good food; grand architecture and fine art
	Pastoral magic of Northeast Kingdom; beautiful villages of Craftsbury Common and Greensboro; swimming; superlative folk-art gallery; good for fat-tired bicycles
	Covered bridge; magnificent lakes; swimming; two antique soda fountains; gorgeous roads
	Best ridden on a fat-tired bicycle; covered bridge; spectacular mountain views; Stowe, swimming; Ben & Jerry's factory tours
	Suits broad variety of bicyclists; mountain views; historic village; Chester Arthur's birthplace; art, crafts, antiques; solitude and peacefulness
Yes	Swimming; lakeshore riding; big views; museums; good food and handsome redbrick architecture in St. Albans; sweeping farmland
Yes	Lake Champlain islands; 100-mile panoramic views; St. Anne's Shrine; swimming; ice cream shop
	Three covered bridges; exquisite landscape; sweeping mountain views; endless apple orchards; visits Canada

FOREWORD TO THE FOURTH EDITION I can remember bicycling around Vermont many years ago with my wife, Susan. We relied on an earlier edition of John Freidin's classic work, *25 Bicycle Tours in Vermont.* Everywhere we pedaled, we'd come across other couples, stopped at intersections to consult the same oracle. John had liberated us all to consider a new, and far better, way of seeing the Green Mountain State.

Because when you're on a bicycle you notice things. You notice the warp and woof of the landscape, of course. But you also notice what you're wheeling past: 12 miles an hour instead of 40, and the whole state looks different. You can read the menu board outside the little restaurant or actually stop for a historic sign. And of course John goes those signs one better with his detailed and lovely descriptions of the human history and natural glory you're passing.

His first book bred a nationwide phenomenon. From its roots in Vermont, bicycle touring spread, and now there's a *Backroad Bicycling in [Insert Your Place Here].* (In fact, Susan and I, with two other friends, wrote such a guide for the Adirondacks years ago. And guess whom we copied?) But Vermont remains almost uniquely perfect for this kind of riding.

Some of that unique bicycling perfection is natural, and some is human. Because Vermont was a farm state, there's a network of back roads that once carried food to market. In this book they become journeys into a lovely past. Vermont, too, has managed to stave off more of the big box stores and fast food strips than most places, which means it's almost always still possible to find a country store for a bottle of chocolate milk and a doughnut. In fact, what most visitors notice is the scale of the state, very different from the suburbanized sprawl that makes up so much of America.

As gas prices have soared, more and more Americans have rediscovered bicycling as a way of getting around. In fact, Americans bought more bicycles than cars in 2005 for the first time in a very long while. But the utility of the bicycle can't disguise the sheer pleasure of riding. For most of us there's something reminiscent of childhood when we swing a leg across the bar and mount up. So I imagine that bicycle touring will boom as well—it is both more sophisticated than auto travel, in that you actually get to see a community, and more youthful. And with John Freidin as your guide, there's almost no way to go wrong.

—Bill McKibben, author of *Wandering Home: A Long Walk Through America's Most Hopeful Landscape: Vermont's Champlain Valley and New York's Adirondacks*
Ripton, Vermont

FOREWORD TO THE FIRST AND SECOND EDITIONS When I think of bicycle touring, I think of Vermont. When I think of bicycle tours, I think of John Freidin.

I can recommend this book so highly because I've worked with John for years and know he knows a great deal about selecting and road-testing tours. You can be assured that these tours will take you to the heart of Vermont.

As an experienced cyclist, John has made sure to guide you to places that will add miles of pleasure to your recreational cycling. If you want to shop, swim, or rest during your tour, this book will tell you where. Perhaps most important, *Backroad Bicycling in Vermont* presents the essence of bicycle touring: traveling under your own power to beautiful places at a pace that suits you. That is the ultimate in independence.

—James C. McCullagh
Former Editor and Publisher, *Bicycling Magazine*

INTRODUCTION

May the road rise to meet you.
May the wind always be at your back.
May the sun shine warm upon your face,
And the rains fall soft upon your fields.
Until we meet again, may God hold you
in the hollow of his hand.

—A Gaelic Blessing

Caterpillars and butterflies. On a ride one day, it struck me that bicyclists could be either one. The difference is their view of the terrain. To caterpillars every hill looks like a mountain, while to butterflies even mountains look flat as they float over them. But given time every caterpillar becomes a butterfly. This is the great marvel of bicycling: Anyone in good health can become a good cyclist simply by doing it. This book is for both caterpillars and butterflies.

Vermont is a bicyclist's paradise not merely because of its beauty, but because of its scale and temperament. Here, we still live in villages, not cities; travel on roads, not highways; and shop at stores, not malls. The people we see on the street are people we know, and our environment is scaled to human proportions. Seldom do more than 10 miles separate general stores; rarely does a climb remain arduous for more than 2 miles. The pace of Vermont life more closely resembles the speed of a bicycle than that of an automobile, and the friendliness of the people is more akin to the cooperation of tandeming than the competitiveness of motoring.

To bicycle is to steep yourself in an environment; to do so in Vermont is to fall in love with both the place and the pedaling.

WHAT THIS BOOK WILL DO FOR YOU This new edition of *25 Bicycle Tours in Vermont*—now more accurately titled *Backroad Bicycling in Vermont*—will:

- Guide you to the most beautiful roads and interesting places I've discovered in more than three decades of bicycling in Vermont.
- Enable you to find your way with confidence.
- Lead you to rides that match your ability.
- Inform you about hills and road conditions before you reach them.
- Increase the pleasure of your ride by telling you a little about the history, architecture, geology, wildlife, and other curiosities along the way.
- Let you know where to find good food, lovely places to swim, and, if necessary, someone to repair your bicycle.

I selected these 25 tours for their beauty and quiet roads. Each had to be beautiful. Each had to use back roads, low on traffic. And, together they had to cover the entire state and match the full range of cyclists' abilities.

Since I wrote the last edition in 1995, traffic on some roads has increased too much. But many back roads have been paved, and I have used these roads to replace or make major revisions in 12 tours and to improve all the others.

The 25 tours in this edition cover more than 1,000 miles and range in length from 16 to 50 miles. Many—especially those in numerical sequence—can be easily combined to create much longer rides. In terrain, the rides vary from nearly flat to very hilly. Three cross into New York, two into New Hampshire, and one into Canada. You can fully enjoy most tours on a narrow-tired bicycle; a few are best on a fat-tired bicycle. Every tour ends where it begins.

SELECTING A TOUR From the state map on page 10, see which tours fall in an area you find interesting or convenient. Then look at the table starting on page 14 to find out which tours offer features you prefer: paved roads, swimming, covered bridges, art galleries, great eating, etc.

Finally, read the tours you are considering and choose which sound best to you.

These 25 tours present far more than 25 choices. Many have side trips or shortcuts. And no tour is the same ridden in one season as it is in another, ridden with friends as ridden alone, ridden in the rain as ridden in the sunshine, ridden when leaves are on the trees as ridden when the trees are bare. Once you know a ride in one direction, try it in the other.

The round-trip mileage(s), difficulty of the terrain, and amount of any unpaved roads are stated at the beginning of each tour. Terrain is rated according to the length, grade, and frequency of hills. But remember, every tour completes a circle, so every inch of climbing is matched by an inch of descent. Here is what the ratings mean, but never be intimidated. Just allow yourself plenty of time.

- Easy terrain is generally level and never requires more than 1.5 miles of uphill riding every 25 miles.

- Easy-to-moderate terrain is also generally level but requires 1.5 to 3 miles of climbing every 25 miles and brings some moderately fast descents.

- Moderate terrain necessitates 3 to 6 miles of ascent for each 25 miles and is best ridden on a bicycle with a low gear in the mid-40s or lower.*

- Moderate-to-difficult terrain requires climbing 3 to 6 miles every 15 miles, and the grades are likely to be steeper than on moderate terrain. A low gear in the 30s is helpful.

- Difficult terrain also requires 3 to 6 miles of climbing for each 15 miles of riding, but the hills are often steep. Gearing in the low or mid-30s is desirable.

PREPARING FOR A TOUR The best way to prepare for a bicycle ride is to bicycle. Other sports such as swimming and running help, but they do not place identical demands on your body. To build your stamina, bi-

---

* To determine that lowest gear on your bicycle, count the teeth on the smallest front chain ring, divide that number by the number of teeth on the largest cog of the freewheel (on the rear wheel), and then multiply the quotient by the diameter in inches of the rear wheel.

cycle frequently and regularly—two or three times a week—and gradually increase the distance and speed you ride. If you hurt somewhere other than your quadriceps, speak with an experienced cyclist to learn whether your pain can be eased by adjusting the height or angle of your saddle, changing it, or wearing different clothing.

VERMONT SEASONS Although April and November bring some wonderful days for bicycling, the principal cycling season in Vermont runs from May through October. I like May and June best because the days are long, the landscape is brilliantly green, and the scents of tree blossoms and flowers sweeten the air. July and August are great for swimming and are rarely too hot or humid. Fall foliage season, covering roughly five weeks from mid-September to mid-October, turns the trees into a riot of color, but the chance of cold or wet days is greater.

Vermont weather is always volatile. From May through August, daytime temperatures can range from 40 to 90 degrees F (4–33 C). During September and October they can go from 30 to 80 F (-1–27 C).

DOING A TOUR When you ride, always wear a helmet and brightly colored clothing. Use a mirror—attached to your handlebars, helmet, or sunglasses—so you can safely see behind you. Make sure your tires are fully inflated, and bring a spare inner tube and pump. Carry water and a little food. Drink before you're thirsty and eat before you're hungry to keep your strength and spirits up.

Read the tour carefully before you start. When you're riding, pause at each turn to review the directions for the next turn; it may come immediately. All roads are paved unless noted otherwise.

Vermont law says that "every person riding a bicycle is granted all rights and is subject to all of the duties applicable to operators of [motor] vehicles, except . . . those provisions which by their very nature can have no application." It also says that cyclists "shall ride as near to the right side of the roadway as practicable." Several regulations govern bicycling after dark, which it is best not to do at all.

To these laws I would add the following recommendations:

- Most important, never make a left turn while you are riding. Stop, get off your bicycle, look for traffic, and walk across.
- Ride single file.

- Do not turn your head to look behind you; your bicycle is likely to curve into the traffic or off the road. Use a mirror instead.

- Do not bicycle across railroad tracks; they can be extremely slippery or catch your front wheel. In either case you're likely to fall.

Although the instructions for each tour mention some potential dangers, do not rely upon their being complete. Road and traffic conditions constantly change. Depend only on yourself for your safety.

Very few cyclists can conquer every hill. But before walking, try this trick. When you reach your lowest gear and can no longer pedal, stop and stand by your bicycle for a minute. Then get back aboard and continue on your way until you need to take another "granny stop." These short stops are guaranteed to relieve your pain by giving your body a chance to reduce the lactic acid that makes your muscles hurt. You can climb nearly any hill more quickly and easily by taking "granny stops" than by pushing your bicycle.

Now, go have fun!

I. SOUTHERN VERMONT

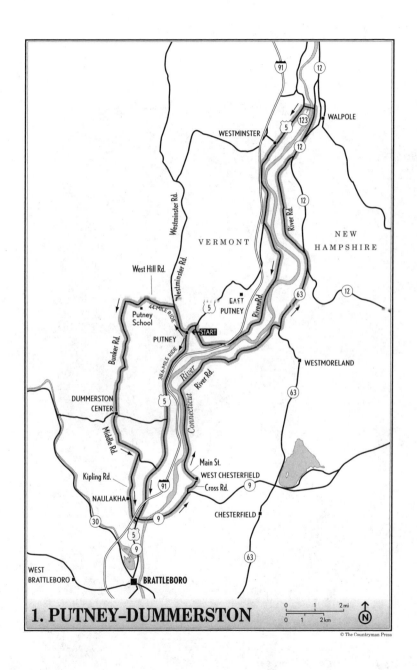

91 12

WALPOLE

123

WESTMINSTER

5

12

River Rd.

12

NEW
HAMPSHIRE

VERMONT

Westminster Rd.

West Hill Rd.

Westminster Rd.

44-MILE RIDE

5

EAST
PUTNEY

63

12

River Rd.

Putney
School

START

Bunker Rd.

PUTNEY

38.6-MILE RIDE

River

WESTMORELAND

River Rd.

63

DUMMERSTON
CENTER

5

Connecticut

Middle Rd.

Kipling Rd.

Main St.

91

WEST CHESTERFIELD

9

NAULAKHA

Cross Rd.

30

9

CHESTERFIELD

5

9

63

WEST
BRATTLEBORO

BRATTLEBORO

1. PUTNEY–DUMMERSTON

0   1   2 mi

0   1   2 km

N

© The Countryman Press

Putney–Dummerston

MODERATE-TO-DIFFICULT TERRAIN; 44 MILES (9.3 MILES UNPAVED)

EASY TO MODERATE; 38.6 MILES (5.9 MILES UNPAVED)

The Putney region abounds with outdoor activity, varied terrain, and striking beauty. This tour focuses on the splendid Connecticut River valley and offers a superb diversity of water scenes, farmland, orchards, and magnificent woods. The longer route begins with 5 very challenging miles, which the shorter route avoids. Both rides follow the same mostly easy terrain for the last 32 miles. Although half of the difficult 5 miles on the 44-mile ride are unpaved, they are fun to ride on either fat or narrow tires.

Putney has a venerable tradition of attracting individuals who are seeking—and in fact create—lives free from many of the conventions of contemporary society. The communes that flourished in Putney and elsewhere during the 1960s and early 1970s had forebears in Putney 130 years earlier. As Ralph Waldo Emerson commented at the time: "The ancient manners were giving way. There grew a certain tenderness on the people, not before remarked. It seemed a war between intellect and affection. . . . The key to the period appeared to be that the mind had become aware of itself."

Putney is widely known for apples (a tenth of Vermont's crop), athletes (Olympians Bill Koch, Tim Caldwell, and Eric Evans), artists (Jim Dine), authors (John Irving and John Caldwell), and, of course, Aiken—the Honorable George—governor, senator, and horticulturist. For years Putney has also attracted skilled weavers, blacksmiths, cabinetmakers, and other craftspeople; many, such as the Green Mountain Spinnery, have

McIntosh apples in September

studios in or near the village. The Putney Nursery grows the largest selection of wildflowers in the eastern United States. Sacketts Brook, which once turned a dozen waterwheels on its boisterous descent to the Connecticut River, flows through the heart of the village, where there are now an eclectic collection of shops, inns, and gourmet delights.

This tour owes much to my good friends Betsy Bates and Neil Quinn. Betsy led tours for Vermont Bicycle Touring for 15 years and, for many years, she and Neil ran the West Hill Shop, one of Vermont's finest bicycle/ski shops.

DIRECTIONS FOR THE RIDE

0.0 From the U.S. Post Office on Main Street in Putney, turn left onto Main Street (US 5 North).

FOR THE 38.6-MILE RIDE: From the U.S. Post Office on Main Street in Putney, do *not* turn left. Instead turn right onto Main Street (US 5 South).

Ride 0.4 mile and just beyond the Putney Food Co-op (on your right), where you can buy some good food to carry along, bear right to continue on US 5 South. US 5 has considerable traffic, but a wide shoulder most of the way. The first 2 miles go downhill; thereafter it rolls more down than up.

Follow US 5 South 5.7 miles more to the traffic light. There, go straight to continue on US 5; do not turn onto Old Ferry Road. Ride another 0.6 mile to the rotary.

At the rotary, go three-quarters of the way around and turn right onto VT 9 East. From there, resume following the directions from mileage 12.1 below.

One hundred forty years ago John Humphrey Noyes, the son of an upstanding Putney family, decided that humankind was no longer corrupted by original sin. Instead, like the children of the 1960s, Noyes believed all persons might achieve perfection on earth. So Noyes created a community to sustain his beliefs. His followers practiced "Bible Communism": the sharing of all labor and property. "All mine thine, and all thine mine."

Noyes's permissive views of sexuality differentiated him from other Christian socialists of his time. He saw little distinction between owning property and owning persons: "The same spirit which abolished exclusiveness in regard to money, would abolish ... exclusiveness in regard to women and children." Noyes's community practiced "multiple marriage," whereby adults shared both child care and sexual intimacy.

Eventually, even the citizens of Putney objected to Noyes's views, so he and his followers fled to Oneida, New York, where they transformed their religious and social concerns into the aesthetic and commercial interests of the famous silver-plate company they founded.

Looking back on his father's Putney community, one of Noyes's sons recalled a quality of life strikingly similar to the communal life of the 1960s: "The relation between our grown folks had a quality intimate and personal, a quality that made life romantic. Unquestionably the sexual relations of the members under the Community inspired a lively interest in each other, but I believe that the opportunity for romantic friendships also played a part in rendering life more colorful than elsewhere."

FOR THE 44-MILE RIDE:

0.1 Turn left onto Westminster Road so you pass the Putney General Store—a good place for drinks and snacks—on your right.

Westminster Road heads seriously uphill for 0.5 mile.

1.2 Two-tenths of a mile beyond the Putney Central School (on your right—not to be confused with the Putney School, which is 1.4 miles farther along the route), turn left onto West Hill Road, which becomes unpaved in 3.2 miles. West Hill Road becomes Bunker Road in 3.7 miles.

Immediately West Hill Road heads steeply uphill. There is no way to describe the next 1.7 miles as anything but very tough—and extremely beautiful. West Hill Road winds through one of the most beautiful woods in Vermont. Sugar maples over 80 feet high and more than 50 inches in girth run from the road's edge up and down the sides of the nearby hills. From the top you descend 1.5 miles.

One and a quarter miles up the hill, you pass the entrance (on the left) to the Putney School. It is a proudly progressive, private coeducational boarding and day school for 255 students, grades nine through twelve. Life at the Putney School carefully integrates college preparation with work on the school and its small farm: "We harvest our own vegetables, sing Bach together, and live close to the land."

5.5 At the T, turn right to continue on Bunker Road, which is unpaved. It becomes paved in 1.4 miles.

Bunker Road rolls up and down through more spectacular sugarwoods. Keep your speed under control on the descents; they can be steep.

7.1 At the stop sign in Dummerston Center, turn left to continue on Bunker Road.

7.2 At the second stop sign, go straight onto Middle Road so you pass the Dummerston Congregational Church on your right.

In 0.8 mile, Middle Road heads nicely downhill for 0.7 mile, which carry you to the turn at mileage 8.7.

Nobel Prize–winning British writer and poet Rudyard Kipling and his American wife, Carolyn, lived in Dummerston from 1892 until 1896. Some 20 years later he described how he kept warm at 30 below on a winter sleigh ride, which he found "beautiful beyond expression": "A walrus sitting on a woolpack was our host in his sleigh, and he wrapped us in hairy goatskin coats, caps that came down over the ears, buffalo-robes and blankets, and yet more buffalo-robes till we, too, looked like walruses and moved almost as gracefully."

8.3 Do not turn onto Dutton Farm Road. Follow Middle Road straight down the hill.

8.7 While you are still going downhill, turn right onto Kipling Road, which is unpaved for 2.2 miles.

Almost immediately Kipling Road goes uphill for 0.4 mile, then heads downhill through more spectacular woods for 0.8 mile. The road is very good, but there may be some gravel on the surface, so be cautious on the descent.

About a half mile after the descent ends, look carefully on your right for a private driveway, marked by two stone pillars. If you stop there, you can look up the drive at Naulakha (Hindustani for "Jewel beyond Price"), the sage green, shingled fortress where Rudyard and Caroline Kipling lived. Kipling designed the home to resemble a ship and placed his study in the prow. He wrote The Jungle Books *and* Captains Courageous *here and began* Kim *and the* Just So Stories. *On a nearby hill he introduced skiing to Vermont, using skis given him by Arthur Conan Doyle, author of the Sherlock Holmes stories. Landmark Trust USA restored and now owns the estate. The house is not open to visitors, although it may be rented for a minimum of three days. If you are fortunate enough to do so, you'll be surrounded by the Kiplings' furniture and have an opportunity to test your skill on Rudyard's personal pool table.*

10.9 At the crossroad, beside the sign (on your right) for the School for International Training and the Experiment in International Living, go straight downhill onto Black Mountain Road, which is paved but unsigned.

The mile-long descent is steep and in 0.3 mile becomes winding. Ride cautiously.

11.8 At the traffic light, turn left onto Putney Road (US 5 North).

12.1 At the rotary, ride just 90 degrees around and turn right onto VT 9 East, which becomes NH 9 East. Ride on the shoulder of the road; the traffic moves fast.

In 0.3 mile you cross the Connecticut River and enter New Hampshire. The Connecticut rises at the conjunction of the Vermont, New Hampshire, and Canadian borders and flows 412 miles southward into Long Island Sound at Old Saybrook. It is New England's longest river and separates Vermont and New Hampshire for the 235 miles of their common border.

There are 11 hydroelectric water storage or generation dams along the Vermont–New Hampshire section of the river. All but one are owned by the TransCanada Corporation and generate electricity during times of high demand. As a result the water level can change quickly by as much as 12 feet and be hard on aquatic life.

After you cross the river, which is the lowest point on the tour, you climb uphill for 0.5 mile.

14.1 Turn left onto Cross Road. Walk across.

14.5 At the stop sign, go straight to continue on Cross Road.

In 0.25 mile, Cross Road dives down a winding, steep hill.

14.9 At the stop sign, turn left onto Brook Street.

15.0 At the next stop sign, turn left onto Main Street, which becomes River Road.

Main Street/River Road is quiet, shaded, and winding. In 0.2 mile you head downhill. At first the descent is steep. Then it becomes gradual and continues for nearly 7 miles, which are twice interrupted by short, sharp climbs.

In a half mile the Connecticut River is on your left for a mile. In the early spring (April through mid-May), thousands of waterfowl migrate along the river. You may see Canada geese, snow geese, black ducks, wood ducks, scoters, horned grebes, ring-necked ducks, mergansers, herring gulls, and common goldeneyes. Along the way, you pass a marker (on the right) commemorating the spot where in 1761 Moses Smith built the first house in Chesterfield.

22.4 At the intersection with Partridge Brook Road (on your right), go straight to continue on River Road.

23.2 At the yield sign and T, turn left onto NH 63 North. Thereafter, stay on NH 63, which is the main road; do not turn onto the side roads.

NH 63 rolls over two half-mile hills.

25.5 At the stop sign, turn left onto NH 12 North toward Walpole. NH 12 has high-speed traffic. Walk across, and then ride on the shoulder.

26.1 Turn left onto River Road, which goes downhill. Again, walk across.

As you approach the next intersection, you'll be riding downhill around a curve that bends sharply to your right. Go very slowly, for the road may be littered with sand and gravel.

28.0 While you are still going downhill, turn left to continue on River Road, which is unsigned. In 30 yards you pass a sign (on the right) for Great Brook Town Forest.

30.3 At the stop sign, turn left onto NH 12 North, which is unsigned here. Thereafter, ride on the shoulder and stay on NH 12, which is the main road; do not turn onto the side roads.

31.1 At the blinking light, continue.

31.8 Turn left onto NH 123 North toward Westminster, Vermont, and ride back across the Connecticut River. Walk across.

32.2 At the T just after you pass through the underpass, turn left toward Brattleboro and US 5 South. Ride 25 yards up the short hill to the stop sign and turn left onto US 5 South.

In 1775 Westminster witnessed one of the first outbreaks of violence between the New York colonial authorities and the citizens living in what we now know as Vermont. Both New York and New Hampshire claimed jurisdiction over the land between Lake Champlain and the Connecticut River. Neither would honor the land grants made by the other. To preserve their right to land granted them by both authorities, Vermonters convened in Westminster on January 16, 1777, and declared their independence of both New York and New Hampshire. This step soon led to Vermont's separate nationhood and subsequent refusal to join the original 13 colonies when they formed the United States. Not until 1791 did Vermont agree to become the 14th state.

36.6 Turn left onto River Road, which is unpaved.

In 0.2 mile, River Road goes steeply downhill for 0.3 mile. Ride cautiously; the road may be rough here. It then becomes smooth and firm. Do not turn onto any of the side roads. In 2.5 miles, you can see the Connecticut River through the trees on your left. At 39.9 miles, River Road becomes paved and goes uphill for 0.5 mile.

43.6 At the stop sign, turn left onto US 5 South, which is unsigned and goes downhill. Walk across. US 5 becomes Main Street in Putney.

44.0 The U.S. Post Office, where you began, is on your right.

Bicycle Repair Services

Andy's, 165 Winchester Street, Keene, NH (603-352-3410)

Brattleboro Bicycle Shop, 165 Main Street, Brattleboro, VT (802-254-8644)

Burrows Specialized Sports, 105 Main Street, Brattleboro, VT (802-257-1017)

Norm's Ski & Bike Shop, Martel Court, Keene, NH (603-352-1404)

West Hill Shop, Depot Road, Putney, VT (802-387-5718)

2

Arlington–North Bennington

MODERATE TERRAIN; 50.1 MILES (11.1 MILES UNPAVED)

Southwestern Vermont and adjacent New York are Norman Rockwell country. This tour, which avoids the region's busy highways and follows unpaved roads nearly a quarter of the way, is especially fun to ride on a fat-tired bike. But it does not require such a bicycle; I've enjoyed it many times on a touring bicycle with narrow tires. Ride the tour in the fall and then the following spring to see the marvelous differences in the land and trees and to smell the differences in the air.

Following wooded lanes and lush valleys between ridges of the Green and Taconic Mountains, the route offers two covered bridges and countless fine views—from the intimate to the panoramic. If you have time and a fishing license, you can try your luck in some irresistible waters, because for 10 miles you cycle along the famous Batten Kill. You can also swim in that river beneath a red covered bridge by the house where Norman Rockwell lived. The tour takes you to two lovely villages, a display of Norman Rockwell's work, and an extraordinary 140-year-old Victorian mansion, now open as a museum.

Connecticut Anglicans settled Arlington in 1763 to enjoy the amenities permitted by their faith in a more tolerant climate than puritanical Connecticut. Under their influence Arlington became the first Vermont town to take such liberties as raising maypoles and decorating Christmas trees. The St. James Cemetery in Arlington on VT 7A bears witness to the early presence of these Anglicans. One of Vermont's oldest burial grounds, the cemetery contains many curious headstones.

Called Tory Hollow during Revolutionary times, Arlington was a Loyalist stronghold but also briefly the residence of Ethan Allen, whose

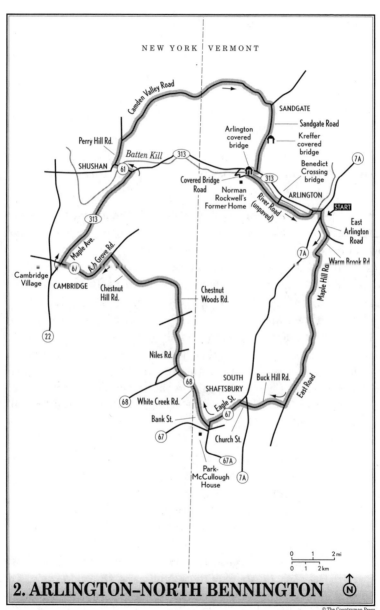

NEW YORK | VERMONT

Camden Valley Road

SANDGATE

Sandgate Road

Arlington covered bridge

Kreffer covered bridge

Perry Hill Rd.

Batten Kill

313

Benedict Crossing bridge

7A

SHUSHAN

61

Covered Bridge Road

313

ARLINGTON

START

Norman Rockwell's Former Home

River Road (unpaved)

313

East Arlington Road

Maple Ave.

A. Grove Rd.

7A

Warm Brook Rd.

Cambridge Village

61

CAMBRIDGE

Chestnut Hill Rd.

Chestnut Woods Rd.

Maple Hill Rd.

22

Niles Rd.

South SHAFTSBURY

Buck Hill Rd.

68

68

White Creek Rd.

Eagle St.

67

East Road

Bank St.

67

Church St.

67A

Park-McCullough House

7A

0   1   2 mi
0   1   2 km

2. ARLINGTON–NORTH BENNINGTON

N

© The Countryman Press

two children and first wife, Mary Brownson, are buried in St. James
Cemetery.

DIRECTIONS FOR THE RIDE

0.0 From the intersection of VT 7A and VT 313 in Arlington, follow VT 7A South
200 yards, and then turn left onto East Arlington Road toward East Arlington.

*Just before you turn, you pass the Norman Rockwell Exhibit on your left. Stuffed into a
former church, the exhibit displays many of Rockwell's Saturday Evening Post covers
and sells reprints. Admission is charged.*

*Rockwell lived in West Arlington from 1939 to 1953. He drew most of his illustrations
of small-town America while he was here, using local citizens as his models. Whether you
like his work or not, it clearly shaped mid-century America's perception of itself.
Describing his 14 years here, Rockwell wrote: "Vermont was an inspiration to my work.
Moving to Arlington had given my work a terrific boost. . . . Now my pictures grew out of
the world around me, the everyday life of my neighbors. . . . I just painted the things I saw."*

*Arlington also became home to Kansas-born Dorothy Canfield Fisher (1879–1958),
the immensely popular chronicler of Vermont life. From 1926 to 1951, she served as one
of the three members of the original selection committee of the Book of the Month Club.
In that role Fisher greatly influenced what Americans read for more than a quarter century. She was also the first woman appointed to the Vermont Board of Education.*

*There are no other places to buy food for 12 miles, so you may want to bring a picnic or
stop at Cullinan's Store, which faces East Arlington Road on your left 100 yards after you
cross VT 7A.*

1.0 Turn right onto Warm Brook Road.

1.7 At the stop sign and blinking light, go straight to continue on Warm Brook
Road, which is unsigned here.

2.1 Turn left onto Maple Hill Road. At its southern end, in South Shaftsbury, this
road is called East Road.

*In 100 yards Maple Hill Road becomes unpaved for 5.5 miles. It goes gently but steadily
uphill for 1.5 miles and then flattens out and descends.*

5.0 Go straight to continue on Maple Hill Road, which is still unpaved and goes
downhill. In 2.2 miles Maple Hill Road/East Road becomes paved.

In 0.1 mile you start up a hill that lasts 1.2 miles and then goes downhill until the next turn.

10.0 Turn right onto Buck Hill Road.

Buck Hill Road tilts sharply upward for 150 yards and then runs rapidly downhill to South Shaftsbury, dropping from a height of 1,200 feet to 740 feet in fewer than two miles.

11.0 At the stop sign and blinking light in South Shaftsbury, go straight across VT 7A onto Church Street.

12.3 Just after crossing the railroad tracks, bear left onto Eagle Street.

14.0 At the stop sign, turn left onto VT 67 West, which becomes Main Street.

14.2 At the intersection beside the redbrick Merchant's Bank (on the right) in North Bennington, turn right to continue on VT 67 West, which now becomes Bank Street.

It is well worth making a 2-block detour here to visit the Victorian Park–McCullough mansion: Instead of turning right, go straight across the intersection and ride 1 block to West Street. Turn right onto West Street and follow it uphill 75 yards to the Park-McCullough House at the corner of West and Park Streets.

Built during the Civil War, this lavish 35-room mansion was designed in the Italianate/Second Empire style, which spoke of power and wealth. The owner, Trenor Park, had grown up poor in North Bennington. He became a lawyer and married a prominent local woman, Laura Hall. In 1851 her father, Hiland Hall—an attorney, scholar, congressman, state Supreme Court judge, and Vermont governor—was sent to California by President Millard Fillmore to settle land claim disputes. At his suggestion, Trenor and Laura Park followed her parents to California in 1852 during the gold rush. Park was no prospector, but he made himself a multimillionaire by managing mines and shrewdly investing in real estate.

Upon returning to North Bennington in 1863, Park built his family a fantasy home, clearly intended to demonstrate his new position. His mansion is organized about a 75-foot central hall, grand stairway, and stained-glass skylight. Its rooms have 14-foot ceilings, parquet floors, Persian rugs, and elaborate marble fireplaces, even though the house was equipped with central heating. The mansion preserves one hundred years of an enormously wealthy family's history and contains more than one hundred thousand items, including outstanding collections of carriages, antique toys, and dolls. A curved drive through the landscaped grounds meanders by formal gardens, outdoor sculptures, a fishpond, a fountain, and a grape arbor. The Park family dog, Abe, even had his own diminutive version of the main house, which later became the children's playhouse.

The McCullough part of the mansion's name derives from Laura and Trenor Park's son-in-law, John G. McCullough, a steamship and railroad magnate who served as both attorney general of California and governor of Vermont. Tours begin daily on the hour, 10–3, mid-May through October. Admission is charged. The grounds and gardens are open from dawn to dusk.

14.5 At the fork, bear right off VT 67 to continue on Bank Street, which is unsigned here and becomes White Creek Road. In New York this road is called County Route 68.

In 2.7 miles, you cross the state line into New York.

18.1 At the 90-degree left curve, go straight off County Road 68 onto Niles Road, which is unsigned.

18.3 At the stop sign and T, turn right to continue on Niles Road.

19.5 At the crossroad, go straight onto Chestnut Woods Road, which is unsigned; in 2.6 miles it becomes Chestnut Hill Road.

In 0.2 mile you pass a sand and gravel pit on your right. In another 0.2 mile you begin climbing for a mile. The first half is steep; the second half is gradual. The grade then turns downward for 3 miles and is often quite steep.

24.2 At the stop sign, turn left onto Ash Grove Road (NY 67 West).

26.6 At the stop sign in Cambridge, New York, turn right onto Maple Avenue (NY 313 East).

To visit the lovely village of Cambridge, New York, where you can find several places to eat and some interesting antiques shops, ride straight at this stop sign onto East Main Street and go 0.5 mile to the stop sign at NY 22. There go straight across NY 22 onto West Main Street and ride another 0.5 mile to the village. After your visit, retrace your way back to the intersection of Ash Grove Road and Maple Avenue (NY 313 East).

32.8 Turn left onto County Road 61 toward Shushan.

33.2 At the stop sign, turn right off CR 61 onto (unsigned) Perry Hill Road.

34.1 Turn right onto Camden Valley Road. Follow the signs for Sandgate and Camden Valley Road for the next 8 miles.

In 0.9 mile you pass an old Moravian cemetery on the right. In 3.9 miles the pavement ends. Camden Valley Road is then unpaved but well packed for 2.5 miles, which slope gently uphill. Immediately after the surface becomes paved again, the road shoots sharply downhill through a series of tight S-curves usually littered with loose gravel. These conditions last 0.8 mile and must be ridden cautiously. After the curves, the road continues moderately downhill for 1.3 miles more.

42.2 At the stop sign in Sandgate, which is merely this intersection, turn right toward West Arlington onto Sandgate Road, which is unsigned.

For the next 3 miles you descend gently, almost without pause, back to the Batten Kill. About halfway down you pass the Kreffer covered bridge on your left. In 1977 designer Susan DePeyster and carpenter William Skidmore converted an open-planked bridge spanning the Green River here into this short covered bridge.

45.3 At the stop sign in West Arlington, which is little more than this intersection, turn right onto VT 313 West, which is unsigned here.

45.7 At the red Arlington covered bridge on your left, turn left onto Covered Bridge Road, which is unpaved and goes through the bridge.

This bridge, built in 1852, stretches 80 feet across the Batten Kill. The swimming below it is excellent. The easiest access is from the far shore.

45.8 At the stop sign and T, turn left onto River Road, which is unpaved.

As you face this T, the house on the right is where Norman Rockwell lived between 1943 and 1954. It is now the Inn at Covered Bridge Green.

47.3 At the first bridge (Benedict Crossing), go straight—do not cross the bridge—to continue on River Road, which is still unpaved. In 2 miles, just before you cross the Batten Kill, River Road becomes paved.

49.4 At the stop sign, just after River Road becomes paved and you cross a bridge, turn right onto Battenkill Drive (VT 313 East), which is unsigned here.

50.1 At the stop sign, you are back in Arlington at the intersection of VT 313 and VT 7A, where you began.

Bicycle Repair Services

Battenkill Bicycle, 1240 Depot Street (VT 11 and VT 30), Manchester Center, VT (802-362-2734)

Eiger of Bennington, 160 Benmont Avenue, Bennington, VT (802-442-8664)

3

Chester–Grafton

EASY-TO-MODERATE TERRAIN; 26.8 MILES (4.6 MILES UNPAVED) PLUS 3-MILE SIDE TRIP

Starting by the long, slender green in Chester, this tour follows rocky streams and maple-shaded roads to some of Vermont's most beautiful architecture. For the cyclist interested in antiques, 19th-century buildings, and local fine art, this tour cannot be beat. There are extraordinary shops and galleries in Chester, Saxtons River, and Grafton, perhaps the most beautiful village in America.

For nearly 5 miles, the route follows unpaved back roads and so completely escapes the nearby busy highways. The views are intimate; the countryside graceful and silent. Along the way are four covered bridges and many splendid old homes built of stone and wood. You may enjoy the unpaved roads best on a fat-tired bicycle, but any bicycle will do fine.

Following small roads along the Williams River, the route comes to an 18th-century burial ground and provides delightful views of small farms and rolling hills. It then turns south along a winding stagecoach road through the woods; you are drawn into the pastoral scene as if no road existed at all. Finally, the tour reaches Grafton, a lovingly restored 19th-century village where you will surely want to linger.

DIRECTIONS FOR THE RIDE

0.0 With your back to the front of the redbrick Chester Art Guild and Chester Historical Society on the Chester green, turn left onto Main Street (VT 11 East).

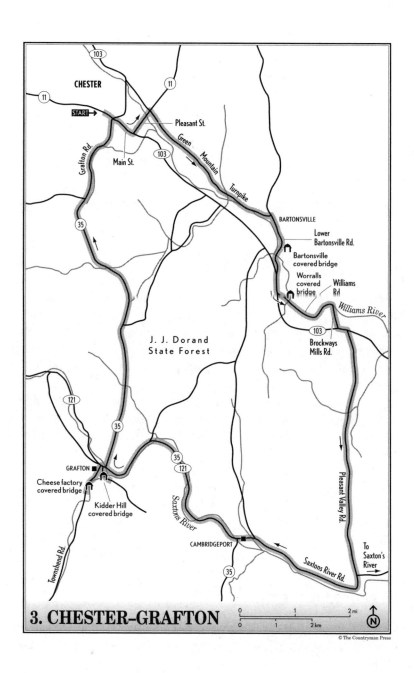

103

11

CHESTER

11

START

Pleasant St.

Green Mountain Turnpike

103

Main St.

Grafton Rd.

35

BARTONSVILLE

Lower Bartonsville Rd.

Bartonsville covered bridge

Worralls covered bridge

Williams Rd

Williams River

J. J. Dorand State Forest

103

Brockways Mills Rd.

121

35

35

121

Pleasant Valley Rd.

GRAFTON

Cheese factory covered bridge

Saxtons River

Kidder Hill covered bridge

CAMBRIDGEPORT

Saxtons River Rd.

To Saxton's River

35

Townshend Rd.

3. CHESTER–GRAFTON

0   1   2 mi

0   1   2 km

N

© The Countryman Press

The Chester Art Guild exhibits the work of local artists, offers classes for adults and children, and sponsors art sales on its lawn.

Next to the Chester Art Guild is a small information booth where you can learn about the area and fill your water bottle. Pick up a copy of A Walking Tour of Chester Village; it's a great way to find the most interesting buildings.

In October 1774, the citizens of Chester were tiring of British rule and at a special town meeting voted "that the people of this town will join forces with their fellow American subjects in opposing in all lawful ways every encroachment on their natural rights."

In the early 19th century, a family of masons named Clark settled in Chester and turned its talents to building stone houses. These gracious homes plus a school and church were constructed between 1838 and 1845 of locally quarried gray green mica schist and secured with mortar reinforced with moss and horsehair. Often a full two-and-a-half stories high, many contain secret hiding places where, before the Civil War, blacks seeking freedom from slavery hid as they fled northward on the Underground Railroad. Most of the stone houses face VT 103, both north and south of its intersection with VT 11. But there are also several along the route.

Chester has restaurants, two nice bookstores, several interesting shops, a general store, and a delightful organic juice and coffee bar called Moon Dog Café. Just 0.5 mile west of the green on VT 11, the Baba-a-Louis Bakery makes and sells wonderful breads and sweet baked goods. It's open Tuesday through Saturday.

0.7 Turn left to continue on VT 11 East.

1.2 At the crossroad, turn right onto Green Mountain Turnpike, which is unsigned and becomes unpaved in 10 yards.

The surface is generally hard and smooth, but occasionally it feels like a washboard. In 0.2 mile you come to Mitchell's 1945 Sugar House on your left. It's the only self-service maple stand I've seen and a delightful, as well as trusting, place to buy syrup.

You are now riding parallel to a footpath established by Native Americans and used later by American colonists as a bridle path and military road. In 1849 the Rutland Railroad Company laid tracks over the path to link Rutland with Boston, thereby creating a new market for Vermont dairy products. The roads are shaded much of the way, lead past beautiful old homes, and cross two covered bridges.

3.0 Turn left toward Bartonsville and continue to follow unpaved Green Mountain Turnpike; it becomes paved in 1.1 miles. If you miss this turn, you reach a railroad crossing in 30 yards.

4.5 At the yield sign, turn right onto Lower Bartonsville Road, which is delightfully narrow.

In 0.7 mile, walk through the Bartonsville covered bridge; it has raised tracks for motor vehicles and could easily cause you to fall. Just beyond the bridge you cross a set of railroad tracks, so ride very cautiously there, too. The Bartonsville Bridge crosses the Williams River and is 151 feet long. Sanford Granger built it in 1870 in the Town lattice style.

5.5 At the stop sign, turn left onto VT 103 South, which is unsigned here. Walk across and ride on the shoulder.

5.7 Turn left onto Williams Road, which becomes unpaved in 0.2 mile and remains unpaved for 1.3 miles. Again, walk across.

The surface of Williams Road is occasionally soft and may have loose rocks on it. You may enjoy it most on a fat-tired bicycle, but you can ride it with any bicycle; it just requires your full attention.

In 0.5 mile, you ride through the unspoiled Worralls covered bridge. Like the earlier covered bridge, this one was built by Sanford Granger in the Town lattice style and

Bartonsville covered bridge (1870)

crosses the Williams River. It is 87 feet long and is remarkable for its pristine condition and lack of signage.

7.2 At the intersection with Gaskill Road/Town Highway 16 on your left, continue straight on the unsigned road, which becomes paved in 20 yards.

7.3 Turn right onto Brockways Mills Road, which is paved but unsigned. You immediately cross the Williams River and then a set of railroad tracks.

7.7 At the stop sign, turn left onto VT 103 South. Walk across and ride on the shoulder.

7.8 Turn right toward Saxtons River onto Pleasant Valley Road.

Pleasant Valley Road climbs gradually uphill for 0.7 mile. In 4.3 miles, you reach the Saxtons River Recreation Area on your left, where you can swim in a nice pond.

3-MILE SIDE TRIP TO THE ROCKINGHAM MEETING HOUSE Instead of turning right toward Saxtons River, ride 1.5 miles south on the shoulder of VT 103. The Rockingham Meeting House (1787) sits on a high knoll on your right, just off VT 103. This two-story clapboard structure is one of the best examples of Federal-style church architecture in New England. Inside are a high pulpit and box pews, each accommodating 10 to 15 people, some of whom must sit facing away from the pulpit. Behind the church lies an old cemetery containing some of the most interesting gravestone carvings in Vermont. They are delicately etched on fragile, weathered slate.

12.6 At the stop sign on the outskirts of Saxtons River, turn sharply right onto VT 121 West.

If you're hungry or would just like to see a lovely, but far less pampered, village than Grafton, turn left onto VT 121 East and ride 0.5 mile to Saxtons River. While you are there, take a look at the 19th-century kitchen and parlor and the excellent collection of old photographs maintained by the Saxtons River Historical Society at the former Congregational Church (1836) on Main Street. The collection is open afternoons from Memorial Day through mid-October on Saturday, Sunday, and holidays.

VT 121 is narrow and winding; it was once a stagecoach road. On the curves, ride carefully near the edge of the pavement, because the bends in the road make it difficult for motorists to see you.

15.5 At the yield sign at the T, in Cambridgeport, turn right toward Grafton onto Chester Road (VT 121 West), which here joins VT 35 North.

19.4 At Grafton, turn right onto VT 35 North toward Chester.

The unique story of Grafton bears telling. Surrounded by low-lying hills at the confluence of the two branches of the Saxtons River, Grafton has ridden the crests of prosperity and the troughs of depression. In the 1820s nearly 1,500 people lived here and thrived on the profits of 13 soapstone quarries and many water-powered mills, including two that loomed the fleece of some 10,000 sheep pastured on the surrounding hillsides. As Grafton flourished, its citizens built fine public buildings, private homes, and a magnificent inn, now called the Old Tavern. With this facility Grafton became a town of distinction, hosting such prominent guests as Ralph Waldo Emerson, Ulysses Grant, Theodore Roosevelt, Woodrow Wilson, and Rudyard Kipling.

Near the end of the century, decline set in. Sheep farmers moved west to find fresh grazing land, and the woolen mills moved south to find cheaper labor. One by one the industries that had produced Grafton's prosperity disappeared. By the end of the Great Depression, fewer than 400 people called Grafton home, and nearly all 80 houses in the village were for sale at rock-bottom prices.

Then, in 1963, thanks to the foresight and generosity of Dean Mathey, Pauline Dean Fiske, and Matthew Hall, the Windham Foundation was born. The purposes of the foundation are "to restore buildings and economic vitality in the village of Grafton; to provide financial support for education and private charities; and to develop projects that will benefit the general welfare of Vermont and Vermonters."

Over the past 40 years the Windham Foundation has bought and rehabilitated many buildings, including the Old Tavern, the Village Store, a dairy farm, the blacksmith's shop, and nearly half of the buildings in the center of the village. To bolster the town's economy, the foundation created the Grafton Village Cheese Company, and to protect open lands, it has gradually acquired 1,900 acres around the village. That land is maintained for wildlife conservation and recreation. This continuing effort has brought Grafton out of a long sleep into a new, but different, life. Jobs have been created, but the success of the foundation has pushed the price of real estate beyond the reach of many former residents. Newcomers have moved in, and some old-timers have left.

But Grafton is no museum town. It is a real village where six hundred citizens live, work, and govern themselves by town meeting. Only a few buildings are open to the public because most are privately occupied, but much of interest is visible from the outside. To guide your exploration, go to the front desk of the Old Tavern and pick up a copy of Walking Tour of Historic Grafton. *It will enable you to find the Grafton History Museum, which has a wonderful collection of antique objects as well as changing exhibits of Grafton's past; the Kidder Hill covered bridge; the Nature Museum, where interactive exhibits will teach you about the area's flora and fauna; the Blacksmith Shop; the Windham Foundation Sheep Exhibit; and the Grafton Village Cheese Company and its covered bridge. There are also many antiques and art galleries. I am especially fond of Gallery North Star, which exhibits and sells original paintings and sculpture by many Vermont artists. The Village Store sells fine sandwiches as well as a good selection of fresh fruit, Grafton cheese, and fudge.*

Upon leaving Grafton on VT 35 North, you climb a steep, heart-pumping hill. After 0.5 mile the slope tapers off to a moderate grade lasting 1 mile. Thereafter, the riding is easy or downhill all the way to Chester.

26.3 At the stop sign, go straight onto Grafton Road, which is unsigned.

26.7 At the next stop sign, turn left onto VT 11 West.

26.8 You are back in Chester beside the green, where you began.

Bicycle Repair Services

Barney's Bike Shop, North Street (VT 103), Chester Depot, VT (802-875-3517)

Lane Road Cycle Shop, 603 Lovers Lane Road, Charlestown, NH (603-826-4435)

Mountain Cycology, 5 Lamere Square, Ludlow, VT (802-228-2722)

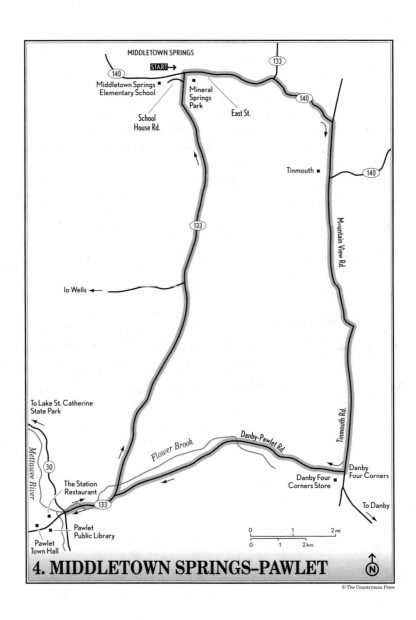

MIDDLETOWN SPRINGS

140

START→

Middletown Springs
Elementary School

Mineral
Springs
Park

School
House Rd.

East St.

133

140

140

Tinmouth

133

Mountain View Rd.

Io Wells →

To Lake St. Catherine
State Park

Mettawee River

30

The Station
Restaurant

133

Pawlet
Public Library

Pawlet
Town Hall

Flower Brook

Danby-Pawlet Rd.

Tinmouth Rd.

Danby Four
Corners Store

Danby
Four Corners

To Danby

0   1   2 mi
0   1   2 km

4. MIDDLETOWN SPRINGS–PAWLET

N

4

Middletown Springs–Pawlet

**MODERATE-TO-DIFFICULT TERRAIN; 28.3 MILES,
PLUS 2.4-MILE SIDE TRIP**

On the western edge of Vermont, not far from Rutland and Manchester, stands a quiet, pristine region of exquisite land and charming villages. This tour explores that region. It is one of Vermont's beautiful, hidden corners, and it used to attract much more attention than, fortunately, it does today. The tour carves a winding path along the edges of hillsides, overlooking small streams, orderly farms, and the maple-covered flanks of the Green and Taconic Mountains. The terrain is alternately challenging, exhilarating, and blissful; the landscape is bucolic. This tour is glorious whenever you do it, but in the fall it is fantastic because tall hardwood trees reach fully across some of the roads. More than any other tour in this book, this one contains glorious descents—and many good climbs, but it is not overwhelmingly difficult.

The tour starts in Middletown Springs, a quiet, remote village of mostly Victorian homes. As it name suggests, Middletown Springs was once a spa. A century ago ladies and gentlemen traveled here by train and horse-drawn carriage to drink and bathe in the healing waters of the iron and sulfur springs. You can visit the reconstructed springhouse and drink as deeply as you like. Middletown Springs also has a wonderful shop that specializes in fine American and European clocks. And later on this ride you can visit the Pawlet Potter, an alpaca farm, and a restored railroad station. If you can, carry along with you food for a picnic; there's little opportunity to buy food until you've ridden nearly 20 . miles.

DIRECTIONS FOR THE RIDE

0.0 From the Middletown Springs green, follow VT 140 East (East Street) and VT 133 North.

Over the next 5.5 miles, you ride from an elevation of 887 feet at Middletown Springs to 1,263 feet at Tinmouth. After a mile of gently rolling terrain, you climb a substantial grade for a half mile. You can buy a snack at Grant's Store on East Street.

In 1772 Native Americans introduced local colonists to the mineral springs along the Poultney River, and soon thereafter legends of the springs' medicinal benefits began to spread among the newcomers. Although the springs played little role in the town's initial development, the population had grown to 1,207 by 1810. It has not been that high since. Then Middletown Springs had four forges, two distilleries, two clothiers, a tannery, five

Middletown Springs green

gristmills, and two cider mills. But the following year, a great flood forced the Poultney River out of its course and buried the springs. When a second flood rerouted the river and uncovered the springs in 1868, a local entrepreneur, A. W. Gray, seized the opportunity. Gray was a successful manufacturer of treadmills that harnessed horses and dogs to generate power. For his new venture he began bottling Middletown's waters and then built the Monvert Hotel, where 250 city folk could stay and "take the waters."

Between 1871 and 1906, horse-drawn carriages brought guests from the Poultney railroad depot to the Monvert Hotel. Once at the hotel, these fortunate visitors dined on caviar and lobster while listening to string orchestras. They played tennis, croquet, and other lawn games. But they came principally to drink and bathe in the waters, which the Monvert claimed could cure "obesity, anemia, nervous dyspepsia, insomnia, diabetes, rheumatism, gout, and nervous troubles." "Nothing," promised the hotel's brochure, "can be more refreshing and exhilarating after a hard ride on the wheel than one of the aforementioned baths and a rubdown by the attendant." What cyclist could argue with that!

The hotel gradually lost its following as travelers opted for locations served directly by railroad coach. Then the Great Flood of 1927 buried the springs once more. For 43 years they remained untouched, until 1970, when local citizens dug out the old spring boxes and built a replica of the Victorian springhouse. The site is charming, if barely suggestive of the grand styles a century ago. The stream is too shallow for swimming, but it makes a delightful place to cool off.

If you would like to fill your water bottle with Middletown Springs water, you can get to Mineral Springs Park by turning right onto Burdock Avenue, which is diagonally across East Street from the town green, and riding 0.1 mile.

2.2 Turn right to continue on VT 140 East.
The first mile goes dramatically uphill, and the second goes equally dramatically down.

5.5 Beside the Tinmouth green on your right, where VT 140 turns left, go straight onto Mountain View Road, which is unsigned here.
The first mile takes you nicely downhill. Thereafter, the terrain is generally easy.

Between the 1780s and 1837, iron was manufactured in the furnace and forges of Tinmouth. That ore and other minerals in the nearby hills probably account for the special properties of the waters in Middletown Springs.

9.0 At the stop sign, turn right onto Tinmouth Road.
You immediately start up a mile-long climb. Then you ride gently downhill all the way to Danby Four Corners.

12.3 At the stop sign in Danby Four Corners, turn right onto Danby-Pawlet Road. Be sure not to go straight, or you will go four miles downhill off the route!

You can get a snack and cold drink at the Danby Four Corners Store. Just beyond Danby Four Corners you must pedal uphill for nearly 1.5 miles, but then you begin a long, beautiful descent that extends nearly without interruption to the next instruction.

18.2 At the stop sign, turn right onto VT 133 North, which is unsigned here.

Within a mile the road turns uphill for a mile. Then the cycling becomes easy for 2.5 miles before climbing another 0.5 mile.

2.4-MILE SIDE TRIP TO PAWLET: If you're ready to eat or would just like to extend your ride with some pretty cycling and a visit to a small village, do not turn right. Instead, continue straight onto VT 133 South, which is unsigned here, and ride 1.2 miles to the next stop sign, which is in Pawlet. VT 133 South is tipped just far enough downhill to make a nice difference.

Set at the convergence of Flower Brook and the Mettawee River, Pawlet prospered as a mill town 150 years ago. At the falls in the center of the village stands a handsome, though idle, waterwheel, 27 feet in diameter and 4 feet wide. During the Depression of the 1930s, Johnny Mach built the wheel to supply his general store and home with electricity. Flower Brook offers excellent swimming just upstream of Johnny Mach's old waterwheel. It is easiest to reach the water from the north side of the river beside the post office. While you are in Pawlet, stop in Mach's General Store to look at the river through the viewing box. You can also get food there.

My first stop in Pawlet is always the studio of the Pawlet Potter, Marion McChesney, opposite The Station Restaurant. Marion is a delightful source of information, and her gracious manner makes every visit a treat. Ask to see her sea stones, her contemporary porcelain in pastel glazes, and her recycled road kills, which are familiar to most cyclists. At The Station Restaurant try a Vermont-made Wilcox rum-and-ginger ice cream cone and look at the railroading memorabilia inside.

If you're curious about alpacas, ride a half mile to Lyn and John Callen's Mettowee Valley Farm. It's an exquisite spot, where the Callens raise multihued, registered alpacas. Ride past The Station Restaurant (on your right), and by the Town Hall (on your right) and the Pawlet Public Library (on your left) for 0.2 mile. Both the town hall and library are worth a look. Then ride across the one-lane bridge and continue another 0.3 mile. The farm will be on your right.

After your visit to Pawlet, retrace your way back up VT 133 North to the intersection where your side trip began. As you know, it is gently uphill all the way. When you reach the intersection, bear left to continue on VT 133 North to Middletown Springs.

23.4 Go straight to continue on VT 133 North; do not turn left toward Wells. *The road continues uphill for 0.3 mile and then becomes easy riding.*

28.2 Just beyond the Middletown Springs Post Office (on your right), you can get to Mineral Springs Park by turning right at the sign for it and riding 0.1 mile. Drink deeply and bring some water and good energy home.

Diagonally across VT 133 from the sign for Mineral Springs Park is School House Road. It's well worth riding 0.1 mile up the hill to see the 1904 wooden Middletown Springs Elementary School, which is still in use.

28.3 At the stop sign, you are back at the green in Middletown Springs, where you began.

Bicycle Repair Services

Battenkill Sports, 1240 Depot Street (VT 11 and 30), Manchester Center, VT (802-362-2734)

Great Outdoors Trading Company, 219 Woodstock Avenue (US 4), Rutland, VT (802-775-9989)

Green Mountain Cyclery, 133 Strongs Avenue, Rutland, VT (802-775-0869)

Sports Peddler, 158 N. Main Street (US 7), Rutland, VT (802-775-0101)

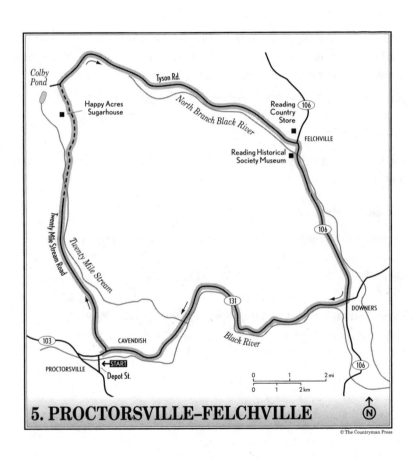

Colby
Pond

Tyson Rd.

Happy Acres
Sugarhouse

North Branch Black River

Reading
Country
Store

106

FELCHVILLE

Reading Historical
Society Museum

106

Twenty Mile Stream Road

Twenty Mile Stream

131

Black River

DOWNERS

103

CAVENDISH

START

106

PROCTORSVILLE

Depot St.

| 0 | | 1 | | 2 mi |
| 0 | 1 | | 2 km | |

5. PROCTORSVILLE–FELCHVILLE

N

Proctorsville–Felchville

MODERATE TERRAIN; 27.2 MILES (3.2 MILES UNPAVED)

Starting in the old mill town of Proctorsville, this tour carves a circle through hardwood forests and quiet farmlands in the Black River watershed. The Black River powered the late-19th- and early-20th-century mills here and nearby in Cavendish and Ludlow. The river is now principally a source of recreation, especially fishing and swimming.

The route is very special for its beauty and its unusual blend of a hearty climb followed immediately by an exhilarating 6-mile descent. The tour's difficult stretch—four miles uphill mostly along an unpaved road—comes at the beginning and is amply rewarded by delightful views of a peaceful valley and the charm of a road canopied by sugar maples. In fact, the abundance of trees makes the ride especially appealing during fall foliage, late September and October in this area. You bicycle nearly the entire way within sight of rivers or streams, and twice have good places to swim. Though the roads suit a narrow-tired bicycle, many riders also enjoy it on a fat-tired bicycle because of the climbing on unpaved roads.

DIRECTIONS FOR THE RIDE

0.0 From the corner of VT 131 and Depot Street in Proctorsville, follow VT 131 East.

0.3 Turn left onto Twenty Mile Stream Road, which is Town Highway 3.

Thereafter, follow Twenty Mile Stream Road straight; do not turn onto the side roads.

Twenty Mile Stream Road immediately starts uphill and quickly gets steep for a mile. Keep an eye peeled for two handsome stone houses. The road surface becomes unpaved at mileage 4.0 and in 0.5 mile turns seriously uphill for 1.5 miles more. The balance of the way has a moderate uphill grade. Although the road surface is hard, it can be rough in places, where loose rocks and washboardlike bumps may occasionally slow you down.

At mileage 6.4 you reach Jim and Sandy Peplau's Happy Acres Sugarhouse on the left. It is an opportune place to rest. The Peplaus are well-known for their graciousness to bicyclists and gladly explain how maple syrup is made and graded. They sell excellent syrup and homemade jams.

7.3 At the T, turn right onto Tyson Road, which is paved and unsigned.

For 0.8 mile Tyson Road too goes uphill, but when you reach the top, you have completed all the climbing on the tour. Tyson Road then turns sharply downhill and carries you along one of Vermont's most exhilarating descents. Slow down. The woods and views are gorgeous, and a stone church and two stone houses pop up along the way. You can also find your own swimming hole in the North Branch of the Black River.

Along the river here and later on the tour, look at the land between the road and the riverbank. These riparian buffers, as they're called, provide the most effective means to protect the water from pollution and invasive species. Vigorous riparian buffers—wide bands of grass, shrubs, and trees—filter pollutants out of human-made runoff. Healthy buffers also create complex ecosystems that provide appropriate habitats for the flora and fauna they shelter. Over the last 20–50 years, natural riparian buffers have been destroyed in many places. Their restoration is vital to future water quality, riverbank stability, and wildlife.

On your way downhill, the lone, high peak in front of you is Mount Ascutney (elevation 3,144 feet).

14.2 At the stop sign in Felchville (Reading PO), turn right onto VT 106 South, which is unsigned here.

Before leaving Felchville, if you are the least bit hungry, go into the Reading Country Store, on your left when you reach this stop sign. The store, which has welcomed hundreds of riders, makes generous sandwiches to your specifications and has good selections of fresh fruit and other groceries. You can picnic on the lawn of the town hall across the street from the store or by the Black River.

The Reading Historical Society Museum, beside the town library on the west side of

VT 106, contains old furniture, clothing, paintings, and photographs. The museum is open by appointment only. Call Laura Griggs at 802-484-5738.

18.4 At the blinking light in Downers, turn right onto VT 131 West toward Cavendish.

In 0.4 mile, if you turn left onto Upper Falls Road, which is unpaved and slightly hidden, and ride 200 yards, you can find a shallow, but pleasant, swimming hole in the Black River. The Black River is a good place to fish for trout. Be sure you have a Vermont license.

Nearly 7 miles west of Downers, just after you have ridden up a short rise that is the only significant incline on VT 131, you come to the tiny village of Cavendish. It has several gingerbread houses and an old stone meetinghouse. Between 1974 and 1994 Alexander Solzhenitsyn and his family were Cavendish's most renowned residents.

27.2 You are back in Proctorsville at the corner of Depot Street, where you began.

Bicycle Repair Service

Barney's Bike Shop, North Street (VT 103), Chester Depot, VT (802-875-3517)

Biscuit Hill Bike & Outdoor Shop, US 4, West Woodstock, VT (802-457-3377)

Mountain Cycology, VT 103, Ludlow, VT (802-228-2722)

Woodstock Sports, 30 Central Street, Woodstock, VT (802-457-1568)

II. CENTRAL VERMONT

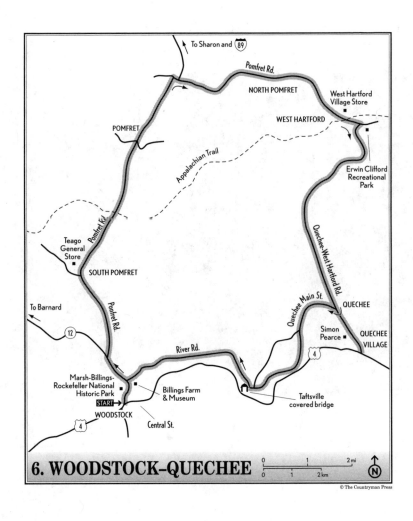

To Sharon and 89

Pomfret Rd.

NORTH POMFRET

West Hartford
Village Store

WEST HARTFORD

POMFRET

Appalachian Trail

Erwin Clifford
Recreational
Park

Pomfret Rd.

Quechee-West Hartford Rd.

Teago
General
Store

SOUTH POMFRET

Quechee Main St.

QUECHEE

To Barnard

Simon
Pearce

QUECHEE
VILLAGE

12

Pomfret Rd.

River Rd.

4

Marsh-Billings-
Rockefeller National
Historic Park

START

WOODSTOCK

Billings Farm
& Museum

Taftsville
covered bridge

4

Central St.

6. WOODSTOCK–QUECHEE

0   1   2 mi
0   1   2 km

N

© The Countryman Press

Woodstock–Quechee

**MODERATE-TO-DIFFICULT TERRAIN; 25.3 MILES
(2.2 MILES UNPAVED)**

This tour begins in Woodstock, one of the most elegant villages in
Vermont. In fact, one 19th-century Woodstock native, U.S. senator
Jacob Collamer, liked to boast, "the good people of Woodstock have
less incentive than others to yearn for heaven." Woodstock's stately

July Fourth Bike Rally, Woodstock, Vermont, circa 1885
THE GEORGE GOODROW MEMORIAL PHOTOGRAPHIC ARCHIVES, THE WOODSTOCK HISTORICAL SOCIETY

19th-century architecture has been so meticulously preserved that all the buildings facing its principal intersection are precisely as they were more than a century ago. The circa 1885 photograph on page 65 depicts a crowd of cyclists and their high-wheeled bicycles standing in front of that unchanged townscape. The villages of Woodstock and Quechee offer lots to see and do, so allow plenty of time to enjoy them both.

Although Woodstock and Quechee often bustle with traffic and pedestrians, this route neatly avoids that commotion by following back roads through the quiet countryside north and east of town. Much of the route follows rivers, and much passes magnificent horse and dairy farms that by Vermont standards are rather pampered. But that takes nothing away from their exquisiteness. The tour includes one difficult climb and one of Vermont's finest downhill runs, nearly seven miles long. Slightly more than two miles at the end of the tour are not paved, but suit narrow- or fat-tired bicycles well.

DIRECTIONS FOR THE RIDE

0.0 From the intersection of US 4 (Central Street) and VT 12 North (Elm Street), follow VT 12 North toward Barnard.

Before leaving, consult the Town Crier Blackboard about special events. The board faces the west side of Elm Street across from Bentley's Restaurant.

Either before beginning the tour or afterward, visit the village. You can get an annotated map at the information booth on the green or at the office of the Woodstock Chamber of Commerce (4 Central Street). Many of Vermont's most distinguished 19th-century Federal homes line Woodstock's oval green and shaded residential streets. Woodstock has always managed to be a center of wealth and gracious living. Though many manufacturing businesses developed along the Ottauquechee River during Woodstock's first hundred years, industry waned after 1850 when the railroad brought out-of-town goods here. Thereafter, finance and commerce, rather than manufacturing, made this town prosperous and kept it beautiful. Perhaps its former wealthy residents shielded Woodstock from change; certainly its most recent residents have tried. Telephone and electrical wires are buried; signs are kept to a minimum. And in 1969, when a new bridge was needed, the town built a 139-foot covered bridge in authentic Town lattice style, using only wooden pegs to hold it together. A team of oxen pulled it into place. In 1974 vandals burned the bridge, and local citizens paid for its faithful restoration. It is formally called Middle Bridge, but locally it is known simply as The Covered

Bridge. Walk or ride through the bridge so you can see the beautiful homes along River Street and Mountain Avenue.

Despite a year-round stream of visitors, Woodstock has none of the garishness that plagues some popular towns. Reserved, urbane, and exclusive, Woodstock's appeal derives from the dignity of its homes and the tastefulness of its galleries and locally owned shops. Four churches—the First Congregational (1807), St. James Episcopal (1907), the Universalist (1835), and the Masonic Temple, formerly Christian Church (1827)—still ring bells cast by Paul Revere.

The Woodstock Historical Society (26 Elm Street) is housed in an 1807 Federal home and exhibits early-19th-century antiques, including furniture, portraits, photographs, silver, farm implements, quilts, toys, and decorative arts. The society is open, mid-May through late October, 10–4 Monday–Saturday and noon–4 Sunday. Admission is charged.

The Woodstock-Quechee area hosts many special events, including a hot-air balloon festival, polo matches, craft exhibits, and concerts. Before leaving town, you might enjoy stopping by F. H. Gillingham & Sons (16 Elm Street). Founded in 1886 as a general store and now selling gourmet foods and hardware, Gillingham's offers a selection that will tempt even the most weight-conscious cyclist. For a fine sandwich go to The Village Butcher, locally known as George's, at 18 Elm Street.

In just a half mile, you come to the Marsh-Billings-Rockefeller National Historic Park (on the left) and the Billings Farm and Museum (on the right). (See mileage 22.1 below for information on the Billings Farm.) The 550-acre park centers about a redbrick Georgian mansion, which was expanded into an extravagant Queen Anne mansion. It was originally the home of George Perkins Marsh, the father of the U.S. environmental movement. Woodstock has a 125-year tradition of genteel environmental consciousness underwritten by deep, deep pockets, and Marsh was part of that tradition. Born into New England's upper crust in 1801 and the son of a U.S. senator, Marsh took up law and served in the U.S. House of Representatives as a Whig (1843–1849), where he opposed slavery and the Mexican War. When Marsh was 48, President Zachary Taylor appointed him minister to Turkey, and in 1861 President Abraham Lincoln made him Ambassador to Italy, a post he held until his death in 1882.

In 1864, while in Italy, Marsh published Man and Nature: Or, Physical Geography as Modified by Human Action. *He had wanted to call it* Man, the Disturber of Nature's Harmonies *but backed off. In 1874 he published a heavily revised edition and gave it a title that more clearly revealed his concern:* The Earth as Modified by Human Action *(1874). Marsh developed his theme by observing the environmental damage caused by*

Vermont farmers. Centuries of dead leaves, naturally composted into the land, had made Vermont abundantly fertile. But by 1820 farmers had squandered those natural nutrients by their aggressive cultivation of grains such as wheat, oats, and barley. Then came the sheep. Vermont farmers cleared nearly every acre of land by 1840 to provide grazing for 2 million sheep. (Today there are roughly 10 million in the entire country!) Marsh's subsequent travel in Europe, which had also begun to devastate its environment, confirmed his observations here.

Unfortunately Americans were not prepared to hear Marsh's message when his books appeared. They were the first modern discussions of ecological imbalance, and in them Marsh compiled an inventory of human assaults on nature. He told of deforestation, canal building, and water pollution. He even showed why the Sahara was expanding. Humans, said Marsh, are not passive inhabitants of earth. They affect its shape and form, and are, therefore, responsible for it and ought to act as stewards, not destroyers. His books were rediscovered in the 1930s and have since come to be regarded as "the fountainhead of the conservation movement."

The Marsh home was most recently the residence of Mary and Laurence Rockefeller, conservationists in their own right, who gave the mansion and its grounds to the national park system. The mansion and a 20-mile network of hiking paths are open to the public daily, May through October. This is the only national park that tells the story of land conservation and of American life on the Vermont home front during the Civil War. It also offers many special programs and events. The mansion itself is magnificent and houses perhaps the finest collection of landscape paintings in the state. They are mostly works of the Hudson River Valley School and include paintings by Albert Bierstadt, Thomas Cole, Frederick Church, and their students.

1.1 Bear right onto Pomfret Road toward South Pomfret.

Over the next two miles the road climbs almost imperceptibly, but nevertheless steadily, as it follows Barnard Brook uphill through an exquisite landscape of gentle(wo)men's farms. The fields are tilled to the tops of the hills and down the sides.

3.1 At the intersection by the Teago General Store in South Pomfret, bear right to continue on Pomfret Road so you pass Teago's on your left.

The Teago General Store sells beverages, cold cuts, cheeses, and breads. Near the store stands the redbrick Abbott Memorial Library, which houses a small collection of local memorabilia.

About a mile and a half from South Pomfret, and later near West Hartford, you cross the Appalachian Trail on its way from Georgia to Maine.

South Pomfret sits at an elevation of 736 feet. Over the next 3 miles you climb nearly 500 feet—sometimes steeply—before reaching the Pomfret Town Hall (on your left) at 1,200 feet. This hill presents the most difficult climb of the tour. From Pomfret you glide downhill 6 miles to West Hartford at an elevation of 420 feet on the banks of the White River.

7.9 At Hewetts Corners, continue straight and downhill on Pomfret Road, which is unsigned here. Do not turn toward Sharon. (Maps of the intersection may be deceptive. The road you follow through North Pomfret to West Hartford is a continuation of the road from Pomfret, while the road to Sharon branches off to your left and goes toward I-89. Some maps make it appear as though the road to West Hartford requires a right turn in Hewetts Corners, but it does not.)

13.0 At the stop sign by the bridge (on your left), turn right onto Quechee–West Hartford Road, which goes uphill and is unsigned here.

If you need a drink or a snack, turn left and ride 0.1 mile across the bridge to the stop sign at VT 14. There, turn left onto VT 14 North and ride 100 yards to the West Hartford Village Store on your right.

If you would like to picnic or swim, the White River is a good spot. One-tenth of a mile up the Quechee–West Hartford Road, turn left onto Westfield Drive and ride 0.2 mile. Then turn left onto Recreation Drive and ride slowly 150 yards downhill to Erwin Clifford Recreational Park. There are picnic tables and toilet facilities at the park, as well as access to swimming in the river.

Over the next 2 miles, the Quechee–West Hartford Road climbs out of the White River Valley, so be prepared for the second and final climb of the tour. Fortunately this climb is dramatically less arduous than the Pomfret climb. From the top the road goes brilliantly downhill for 2 miles.

18.0 You reach the village of Quechee. After your visit, retrace your way 0.9 mile and immediately beyond a turnout and sign for Quechee Lakes, both on your right, bear left onto Quechee Main Street.

Quechee has a small collection of galleries and shops and a tiny covered bridge. It is also the home of the well-known glassblower Simon Pearce. There, in a 200-year-old former woolen mill, you can watch master craftspeople turn molten glass into fine crystal. With its high brick walls, huge windows, and maple floors, the mill itself is a splendid sight. Glassblowing requires an enormous amount of heat; the Ottauquechee River powers the 60-year-old turbine that generates all the power used in the building and a little extra. An elegant little restaurant, overlooking the falls, at Simon Pearce serves fine lunches and dinners.

22.1 At the red, 189-foot Taftsville covered bridge (1836), turn right onto River Road, which is unpaved and unsigned. Do not ride through the bridge. From this turn to the next, find your way by taking the roads that keep the Ottauquechee River on your left.

River Road is smooth, but unpaved, for 2.2 miles. While you could return to Woodstock via US 4, it would be a foolish thing to do. The traffic is heavy, and the road narrow. Although River Road demands attention, it is quiet, shaded, and provides a delightful view of the Ottauquechee.

In 3 miles, just before your next turn, you reach the entrance to the Billings Farm and Museum on your left. This 88-acre farm and agricultural museum reflects the spirit of late-19th-century Vermont agriculture. The farm milks championship Jersey cows, raises Southdown sheep, and demonstrates the use of draft horses and oxen. In the late 19th century, manufactured goods were displacing handcrafted ones, and the railroad was tying local farmers to the markets and manners of the urban Northeast. The Billings Farm reveals the richness and sophistication of Vermont farm life as well as its ordinary details. Explore the barns at milking time, the farm life exhibits, and the award-winning 1890 Farm House. The museum is the creation of Laurence and Mary Rockefeller; Mary's grandfather, Frederick Billings, purchased the farm in 1869 and made it a showcase of advanced farm management. It is open daily 10–5, May through October. Admission is charged.

25.1 At the stop sign, turn left onto VT 12 South, which is unsigned here.

25.2 Just beyond the BAD INTERSECTION AHEAD sign, bear left to continue on VT 12 South (Elm Street).

25.3 You are back in Woodstock where the tour began.

Now consider stretching your legs with a walk along one of the town's short nature trails, either Faulkner or Mount Peg. Maps of both are available free at the information booth on the green.

Bicycle Repair Services

Biscuit Hill Bike & Outdoor Shop, US 4, West Woodstock, VT (802-457-3377)

Woodstock Sports, 30 Central Street, Woodstock, VT (802-457-1568)

7

Brandon–West Rutland

EASY-TO-MODERATE TERRAIN: 36 MILES (1.4 MILES UNPAVED)

A sweet farming valley, a town of white marble, a 140-year-old brick mansion, sweeping views of the Green Mountains, and the historic village of Brandon (where 243 buildings are listed on the National Register of Historic Places) make an ideal tour. The ride slips quickly out of Brandon onto rural roads, nearly free of traffic. The lavish Wilson Castle and Vermont Marble Exhibit will fire your imagination with images and sounds of ways of life and work one hundred years ago. Both fall about two-thirds of the way along the ride and make fine places to picnic and rest.

The tour begins and ends in Brandon, where you can eat a wonderful breakfast, lunch, or dinner indoors or alfresco at Chef Robert Barral's Café Provence. Make time, if you can, to explore Brandon on foot as well. There are two waterfalls, craft shops, antiques stores, an abundance of handsome homes, and several restaurants. The best way to explore the village is to use the *Brandon Historical Village Self-Guided Walking Tour* pamphlet. You can pick up a free copy at the information booth beside the Brandon Public Library, located where VT 73 heads east off US 7. (For more information about Brandon, see the Brandon–
Fort Ticonderoga tour.)

DIRECTIONS FOR THE RIDE

0.0 From the U.S. Post Office in Brandon, turn left onto Pearl Street.

As you make this turn, you will see the Brandon Baptist Church on the west side of US 7.

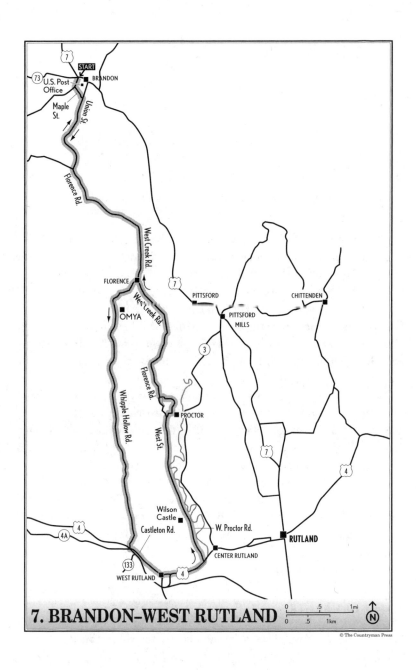

7. BRANDON–WEST RUTLAND

In 1950 a powerful hurricane destroyed the steeples on many of Vermont's churches. This Greek Revival church had withstood storms since 1832, but in 1950 it, too, succumbed. The winds of November 1950 threw the original steeple like a javelin through the roof of the church. Fortunately, no one was in the building at the time. Then, in July 2000, after years of work and fund-raising, a new 50-foot steeple was raised onto the existing 75-foot tower base. The restored steeple, meticulously documented and detailed from historic photographs, tops out at 135 feet. It should be considerably more resistant to lateral wind forces than its unfortunate predecessor. You can see the steeple from miles away in every direction.

You leave Brandon along one of its most beautiful residential streets. The other is Park Street (VT 73), on the east side of US 7.

0.3 Turn left onto Maple Street.

0.7 At the stop sign and T, turn right onto Union Street, which leads through an open valley of small farms overlooked by a panorama of the Green Mountains to the east.

3.1 At the stop sign, turn left onto Florence Road.

In 0.7 mile, Florence Road becomes unpaved for 0.7 mile; the surface is hard and free of rocks, but it does have some loose gravel on it.

Over the balance of this ride, look at the roofs of old houses and barns. Several miles west of here—between Fair Haven and Pawlet—a great belt of slate runs down the Vermont–New York border. That slate has provided countless houses and barns in southwestern Vermont with exquisite, durable roofs. Before World War II, slate, being a local product, was not only the best material for roofing; it was the least expensive.

7.2 At the yield sign, turn right onto West Creek Road.

7.4 Turn right onto Whipple Hollow Road. Do not turn left and ride beneath the railroad bridge.

7.6 Follow Whipple Hollow Road as it curves to the left and crosses the railroad tracks.

You will then pass the west entrance to OMYA. For the next mile there may be some heavy trucks on the road. They are carrying calcium carbonate, which is made from crushed marble, quarried here.

In 0.7 mile you will reach the most difficult climb of the tour. The hill lasts just over a mile. It is followed by several short, rolling hills.

15.9 At the stop sign at the T, turn left onto Castleton Road.

In a mile you will pass on your right the West Rutland High School and then the West Rutland Public Library. Both are made of local quarried Danby white marble.

17.0 At the stop and blinking red light, go straight onto Main Street.

17.1 Bear left to continue on Main Street (VT 4A East). Beware of traffic on VT 4A. Do not turn right onto VT 133 South unless you wish to link this ride with the Middletown Springs–Pawlet ride or just want to add some beautiful cycling.

17.3 Where VT 4A ends, continue straight onto US 4 (Business) East. Again, be very careful of the traffic.

18.6 Stop and walk carefully across US 4 (Business) and begin riding north on West Proctor Road toward Wilson Castle. In 1.2 miles West Proctor Road becomes West Street.

Wilson Castle will be on your left in 0.9 mile. It is well worth a stop. A local physician, John Johnson, had the castle built between 1867 and 1874. Johnson spent most of his career practicing medicine in England, where he met and married a wealthy English patient of his, Sarah Robbins. Her fortune paid for the castle, but two years after its completion she left both the castle and her husband.

The castle takes its name from Col. Herbert Wilson, who bought the property in 1939. Wilson had made a fortune as an early pioneer in the radio industry. There is still a working broadcast antenna across the road from his castle. The fifth generation of his family occupies part of the castle during Vermont's warm months.

Wilson Castle and its elaborate European and Oriental furnishings demonstrate how America's most wealthy and ostentatious families lived 130 years ago. The excesses of those times were unrivaled until the past decade in the United States. The castle is a potpourri of European architectural styles. Nineteen open proscenium arches, a towering turret, a parapet, and a balcony dominate the brick and marble façade. Inside are 32 high-ceilinged rooms, 13 fireplaces of imported tile and bronze, and 84 stained-glass windows. Admission is charged; guided tours take about 45 minutes. You may picnic on the grounds for free.

23.0 At the intersection beside the West Street Market (on your right), bear right onto Cross Street.

West Street Market will make you a sandwich to order.

Wilson Castle

23.1 At the stop sign, go straight onto the unsigned road, which becomes Market Street, so that you pass Proctor Gas, Inc., on your right.

23.3 At the stop sign, go straight across the five-legged intersection onto High Street.

You enter Proctor beside the marble sheds of the Vermont Marble Company, now owned and operated by OMYA, a gigantic Swiss conglomerate. OMYA quarries most of its marble to pulverize it into fine-ground calcium carbonates, which are used in everything from paint to plastics, toothpaste to Tums.

Proctor grew up as a company town. Its location beside a forceful river, the Otter Creek; one of the world's largest marble belts, which runs from Middlebury to Manchester; and a railroad line made Proctor an ideal place for the marble business. Proctor took its name from Col. Redfield Proctor, who founded the Vermont Marble

Company in 1880. Using the Otter Creek to power saws and grinding stones and the local railroad to export the finished product, Proctor built his company into one of the largest corporations in the world. Several thousand people from nearby towns and Europe came to work for the company. In the course of its life, Vermont Marble acquired rights to all the marble deposits in Vermont, Colorado, and Alaska and became the giant of its industry.

The town still sparkles with marble sidewalks; a marble church; a marble cemetery, gathered about Redfield Proctor's marble mausoleum; and an exquisite marble bridge over the Otter Creek. Colonel Proctor was elected governor of Vermont and then a U.S. senator. As chair of a committee that oversaw federal construction projects, Senator Proctor made certain that Vermont marble was used to build the Jefferson Memorial, the U.S. Supreme Court, and the Senate Office Building. Later the United Nations Secretariat in New York City was constructed of white Vermont marble.

23.6 The Vermont Marble Exhibit is on your left. After your visit, turn right out of the driveway onto High Street and retrace your way back to the five-legged intersection.

The exhibit is an archive of a company town, a geological classroom specializing in marble, and a gallery of marble sculpture. You will find bas relief carvings of every U.S. president and polished examples of all the varieties of marble quarried here. A short walk from the museum takes you to the original Sutherland Falls quarry, now inactive. It is now filled with water and hauntingly beautiful: steep white marble walls, gleaming depths, and silence.

To see the village of Proctor, continue straight 0.1 mile past the Vermont Marble Exhibit to the T. There, turn left onto Main Street and ride another 0.1 mile across the marble bridge to the next T. There, turn right onto South Street. Ride 0.3 mile and the Proctor cemetery, where Redfield Proctor is interred, is on your left.

23.7 At the stop sign at the five-legged intersection, turn right onto North Street.

24.0 Bear left onto the unsigned road, which goes gently uphill for 0.2 mile and becomes Florence Road.

24.1 Turn left onto Florence Road. In 0.4 mile you will pass the northern end of Beaver Pond.

The road runs gently uphill for a mile and then down a hill, which becomes winding and steeper as you go. Along the way beware of gravel on the road, especially on the curves. The descent lasts 1.7 miles.

28.5 At the stop sign, immediately after you pass beneath the railroad overpass, bear right onto West Creek Road. You will now retrace your way back to Brandon. See how fresh it looks when you're riding in a different direction.

28.9 Bear left to continue on West Creek Road; do not turn toward US 7. *In 0.8 mile, West Creek Road becomes unpaved for 0.7 mile.*

32.8 Turn right onto Union Street.

35.2 Turn left onto Maple Street.

35.7 At the stop sign, turn right onto Pearl Street.

36.0 At the stop sign, the U.S. Post Office in Brandon is on your right.

Bicycle Repair Services

Alpine Shop, Merchants Row, Middlebury, VT (802-388-7547)

The Bike Center, 74 Main Street, Middlebury, VT (802-388-6666)

Great Outdoors Trading Company, 219 Woodstock Avenue (US 4), Rutland, VT (802-775-9989)

Green Mountain Cyclery, 133 Strongs Avenue, Rutland, VT (802-775-0869)

Sports Peddler, 158 N. Main Street (US 7), Rutland, VT (802-775-0101)

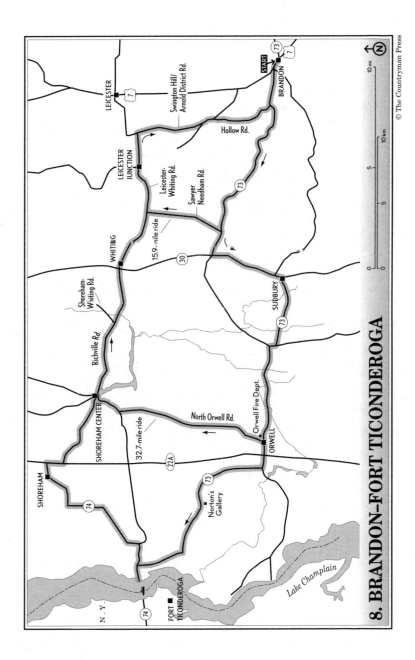

© The Countryman Press

8. BRANDON–FORT TICONDEROGA

Brandon–Fort Ticonderoga

EASY-TO-MODERATE TERRAIN; 15.9 MILES (3.2 MILES UNPAVED)

MODERATE TERRAIN; 32.7 MILES (1.9 MILES UNPAVED)

MODERATE-TO-DIFFICULT TERRAIN; 45.8 MILES (1.9 MILES UNPAVED)

The different lengths of the three rides offered by this tour—and the differences in the terrain of each—make it ideally suited for a group of cyclists of varying abilities. The 45-mile tour merits a moderate-to-difficult rating because the ride in New York State to Fort Ticonderoga and the ride from Lake Champlain back to Brandon both gain considerable elevation.

Revolutionary history, apple orchards, prosperous dairy farms, and panoramic mountain vistas characterize this ride through the southern Champlain Valley, "Land of Milk and Honey." To maximize the superlative long views of the Adirondacks and Green Mountains, ride the route on a clear day. Leaving Brandon and then twice crossing the Otter Creek, an important Native American travel route two hundred years ago, you cycle parts of the old Crown Point Military Road, which Lord Jeffery Amherst cut through the wilderness from Charlestown, New Hampshire, to Lake Champlain in 1759. During the winter of 1775, Col. Henry Knox and his army of farmers hauled 59 cannons over this road all the way from Fort Ticonderoga to Boston. There George Washington's army used them to help expel the British.

Along the first 6 miles of the ride are several antiques shops. The longer ride also takes you across Lake Champlain on a tiny ferry to Fort Ticonderoga and to the splendid Norton Gallery, where scores of wooden animals are carved and sold by sculptor Norton Latourelle.

Brandon is a good place to browse and to eat. Three of my favorite spots are the gallery of the Brandon Artists Guild at 7 Center Street, Briggs Carriage Bookstore at 16 Park Street, and Café Provence at 11 Center Street. (For more information on Brandon, see the Brandon–West Rutland tour.)

DIRECTIONS FOR THE RIDE

0.0 From the Historic Brandon Baptist Church at the intersection of US 7 and VT 73 in Brandon, follow VT 73 West.

In 1.7 miles, the Otter Creek, Vermont's longest river, pulls along the south side of VT 73. It will be in sight for much of the next 1.8 miles. There's one hearty climb of a mile about 3.7 miles after you leave Brandon

Brandon was chartered in 1761, and fine post-Revolutionary and Victorian homes line its wide streets. Stephen A. Douglas, "The Little Giant," who in 1860 ran for president as a Democrat against Abraham Lincoln, was born here in 1813 in a story-and-a-half cottage. It sits at the northern end of the village, on the west side of US 7, and now serves as the headquarters of the local Daughters of the American Revolution. It is only irregularly open to the public.

Douglas and Lincoln differed not about the abolition of slavery—in 1860 neither favored abolition—but about whether slavery should be legal in U.S. territories. Douglas and the Democrats favored allowing the voters in each territory to decide by ballot whether or not to permit slavery. Lincoln and the Republicans advocated Congressional legislation to prohibit slavery in the territories. Neither position suited the eight cotton states, which, following the lead of Jefferson Davis, withdrew from the Democratic Party and nominated their own presidential candidate, John C. Breckinridge, then the vice president. With the Democrats split, Lincoln won a sound electoral victory (59 percent), though he received only 40 percent of the popular vote.

Vermont was the first state in the United States to prohibit slavery; Vermont took that step in 1791. In 1860 Vermont voted four to one for Lincoln over its native son Douglas.

FOR THE 15.9-MILE RIDE   Follow VT 73 West only 5.4 miles—there's one hearty climb of a mile about 3.7 miles after you leave Brandon—and then turn right onto Sawyer-Needham Road.

Follow Sawyer-Needham Road 2.5 miles to its end. Sawyer-Needham Road is unpaved and rough for 100 yards, and then it becomes paved for 1.2 miles. The pavement was in bad repair in August 2005, but despite its poor surface, Sawyer-Needham Road will

charm you. It is tiny, has virtually no traffic, and leads past well-tended farms and a mag-
nificent view of the Green Mountains.

After the paved portion, Sawyer-Needham Road becomes unpaved once again until
it ends at a stop sign and T. There turn right onto Leicester-Whiting Road and follow it 2.2
miles to the stop sign and T. There resume following the directions below from mileage
40.0.

6.2 At the stop sign, turn left onto VT 30 South, which is also VT 73 West. Ride
very carefully along this part of the route, for the traffic goes fast.

For a mile VT 30 is flat. Then it goes uphill for a mile, which ends at the Sudbury Congre-
gational Church on your left. From the church VT 30 starts down a steep hill. Go slowly,
because in 0.2 mile you must turn off VT 30 on the steepest part of the descent.

8.5 Turn right onto VT 73 West, which goes rapidly downhill for 0.4 mile and
then gently downhill for 0.5 mile before opening into a broad farmland valley.

The next 5 miles provide solid evidence of the adage: "Vermont ain't flat!" You ride up and
down five rolling hills, each no more than a half mile long. At the Orwell Fire Department
on your right, you start the final descent, which is steep and winding.

FOR THE 32.7-MILE RIDE Two tenths of mile beyond the Orwell Fire
Department—and just 0.1 mile before the Orwell green—turn right onto North
Orwell Road and follow it 5.5 miles to its end. It is a lovely, quiet back road that
meanders past a series of dairy farms and broad fields of trefoil, clover, and
corn. North Orwell Road is also easy riding, although you do encounter two
short climbs of less than a half mile each.

Beware that North Orwell Road ends at a stop sign as you are going downhill. You will
know the stop sign is just ahead when you can see a lake on your right. At the stop sign,
turn right onto Richville Road, which is unsigned at this intersection; you will immediately
cross a bridge at the north end of Richville Pond.

Follow Richville Road—which becomes Shoreham-Whiting Road—4.1 miles to the stop
sign and crossroad at Whiting. There, resume following the directions below from
mileage 36.4.

13.7 You reach the shaded Orwell town green on your right. It's a good spot to
picnic or rest within sight of the redbrick First Congregational Church (1843)
and white town hall, built in 1810 as a Baptist church. If necessary, you can get
under cover in the bandstand. Stop by Buxton's Store to get a snack or just to
see an authentic Vermont country store.

The Orwell Town Hall, as seen through the bandstand

During the middle of the 19th century, Orwell became prosperous as a center of Vermont's vigorous wool industry. In the 1830s Merino sheep were the state's principal livestock, and most of the state was cleared for their pasture. Though sheep raising faded in Vermont after the Civil War, it is now enjoying a modest revival.

14.0 At the stop sign and blinking light, go straight across VT 22A to continue on VT 73 West. Do not bicycle on VT 22A; it has far too much high-speed traffic, especially trucks.

14.4 At the yield sign, bear right to continue on VT 73 West toward Fort Ticonderoga.

Over the next five miles you go mostly downhill. The Adirondacks fill the western horizon, Lake Champlain comes into view, and finally the red roofs of Fort Ticonderoga emerge from the crowns of the trees.

Less pleasing is the sight of dense smoke emerging from the enormous smokestacks of the International Paper plant in Fort Ticonderoga. As of the fall of 2005, International Paper was several years into its effort to receive permits from the State of New York and the federal Environmental Protection Agency to burn 72 tons of shredded tires a day. Prevailing winds blow from the west and consequently would spread smoke from the burning tires across Vermont and perhaps New Hampshire and Maine, which have no authority to regulate the plant. Many citizens from Vermont are outraged by the potentially harmful effects of the particulates in the smoke. As seven-year-old Autumn Sombric of Bridport said, "Why aren't we allowed to burn our trash in our barrels when they are allowed to burn tires?"

A little more than five miles beyond VT 22A, you will find Norton's Gallery on your left. I call it the home of the big dogs! Norton Latourelle has been making wonderful whimsical woodcarvings for 30 years. He is perhaps best known for his dogs, which can be as tall as 8 feet. Norton has carved more than 70 breeds, as well as many sorts of cats, birds, other animals, and flowers. He does all the work himself—from design to carving to coloring. Small pieces are whittled, and larger ones are carved from thick planks of local white pine. Norton is a self-taught artist, and his work has been displayed in galleries throughout the United States. His gallery is open most days and by appointment (802-948-2552). It is a most delightful place to visit and has a spectacular view to the west.

20.1 At the stop sign and T, turn left onto VT 74 West toward Larrabees Point and head downhill to the lakeshore. Keep your speed down.

20.7 At Larrabees Point, stop to take the tiny Shorewell Ferry across Lake Champlain. After disembarking on the New York side, go straight onto NY 74 West, which goes steadily uphill for 0.6 mile to the entrance to the fort.

The 60-foot excursion boat Carillon also departs from Larrabee's Point. It offers hour-and-a-half afternoon cruises four days a week during July and August; it's a lovely trip. Call 802-897-5331 for a schedule and prices. The Carillon was built in 1990 in the style of a 1920s Thousand Island luxury cruise boat. Capt. Mahlon Teachout provides a lively commentary as he recalls local yarns and Revolutionary history.

The Shorewell Ferry (802-897-7999), which has been running for more than two centuries, operates between 8 and 7. It is guided across the lake's currents by an underwater cable. The crossing takes 7 minutes, so you should not have to wait more than 15. Cyclists are welcome and are charged about $3 round trip.

After the five Great Lakes, Champlain, covering 435 square miles, is the largest body of fresh water in the United States. Long and narrow, it begins 35 miles south of

Larrabee's Point and stretches northward 136 miles, the last 18 falling in Canada. At its widest point, north of Burlington, the lake measures 15 miles across, but most of it is much narrower. In winter it often freezes to a depth of 22 inches—enough to support cars and light trucks as well as ice fishers. Champlain is one of the few lakes in North America that flows northward; it empties into the St. Lawrence River. A series of 12 locks and a canal near Whitehall, New York, connect the lake at its southern end to the Hudson River.

21.3 At the sign for Fort Ticonderoga, turn left and follow the mile-long driveway to the fort. After your visit, retrace your way back to the ferry and return to Vermont.

Between mid-May and mid-October, from 9 to 5, visitors are welcome at Fort Ticonderoga, a National Historic Landmark. Admission to the fort and its fine military museum is well worth the charge. A restaurant and large picnic area are located outside the stockade and are accessible without charge.

Militarily, the fort was the key to Lake Champlain because it protected the portage between Champlain and Lake George to the south. Originally named Fort Carillon, the fort first served the French, who built it, then the British, the Revolutionary colonists, and the United States.

In July 1758, British general Abercromby unsuccessfully led 16,000 British and colonial troops against a French force of just 3,200. The Battle of Carillon lasted only hours, but Abercromby lost more than 1,900 soldiers.

A year later, the British, now led by Gen. Jeffrey Amherst, again attacked Fort Carillon. This time, after a four-day siege, the French abandoned the fort and blew up their powder.

Sixteen years later, in 1775, Ethan Allen and Benedict Arnold independently concluded that the adjacent British forts at Ticonderoga and Crown Point, New York, made easy targets. Their goal was to capture the cannons from both forts. In the early-morning darkness of May 10, 1775—just three weeks after skirmishes at Lexington and Concord heralded the Revolution—83 Green Mountain Boys led by Allen and Arnold rowed across Lake Champlain. They surprised the sleeping sentry, stormed the fort, and quickly captured it from a small British garrison, which later also surrendered Fort Crown Point. That winter Col. Henry Knox led an expedition that dragged the cannons from Fort Ticonderoga and Crown Point over the snow to Boston. Gen. George Washington's army used them to free Boston from British occupation.

In 1776, while commanding Forts Ticonderoga and Crown Point, Benedict Arnold oversaw the construction of the first American navy. The fleet was built to thwart a British *invasion from Canada. That winter the defenses at Ticonderoga were expanded to include a fort across the lake at Mount Independence and a floating bridge to connect the two fortifications. In October, Arnold's fleet engaged the British navy in the Battle of Valcour Island, some 70 miles north of Ticonderoga. The superior British navy decimated Arnold's fleet but withdrew to Canada in anticipation of winter.*

23.9 From the ferry landing at Larrabees Point, go straight uphill on VT 74 East.

Over the next four miles you climb from an elevation of 95 feet at Lake Champlain to 396 feet at Shoreham. Most of the climb is gradual.

24.4 Go straight to continue on VT 74 East, which becomes Main Street in Shoreham.

In 4.5 miles, as you crest the final hill into Shoreham, you reach the outstanding Lapham and Dibble Gallery on your left at 410 Main Street. The gallery restores and sells fine American paintings and prints and is definitely worth a visit. It's usually open 9–5 Tuesday–Friday.

Shoreham sits at the heart of Addison County's apple-growing district. Although more McIntosh are grown here than any other variety, scores of varieties are raised in Addison County. From Shoreham, the ride gains another 100 feet before you reach Brandon.

28.9 At the stop sign and T, turn right onto VT 22A South toward Orwell. Ride very cautiously, for there may be trucks on the road.

29.9 Turn left onto Richville Road toward Shoreham Center and Whiting. Be sure to walk this turn.

You will climb for a gentle half mile and then enjoy a mile-and-a-half descent. Thereafter, the road crosses two small hills and then descends another mile and a half. The views of the Green Mountains are stupendous.

36.4 At the stop sign and crossroad at Whiting, go straight across North Main Street (VT 30) onto Leicester-Whiting Road.

Just before you cross North Main Street, look leftward at the Whiting Community Church, built in 1811. In May 1775, when Ethan Allen wanted to gather the Green Mountain Boys for their attack on Fort Ticonderoga, he dispatched Whiting blacksmith Samuel Beach as his messenger. The hardy Vermonter ran 64 miles in 24 hours to summon the backwoods clan for its sally across Lake Champlain.

In a mile and a half you begin the first of two descents. The first lasts 0.8 mile; the second is short, but it must be ridden slowly since it ends by crossing a double set of railroad tracks.

40.0 At the stop sign and T, turn right onto Swinington Hill Road—which almost immediately goes up a hill for 0.6 mile—toward Brandon. At the top you have a splendid view of the Adirondacks on your right. Swinington Hill Road then becomes Arnold District Road.

43.0 Bear right onto Hollow Road, which is unpaved, shaded, and wonderfully narrow. It also enables you to avoid cycling on US 7.

Hollow Road is the sort of road that virtually disappeared from Vermont nearly 50 years ago, but it fortunately still exists in England, Scotland, and Ireland. The surface is hard and mostly free of rocks; just go slowly on the downhill portions.

44.9 At the stop sign and T, turn left onto VT 73 East, which is unsigned here. In a few minutes you will see the spire on the Brandon Baptist Church.

45.8 You are back in Brandon beside the Brandon Baptist Church, where you began the ride.

Bicycle Repair Services

Alpine Shop, Merchants Row, Middlebury, VT (802-388-7547)

The Bike Center, 74 Main Street, Middlebury, VT (802-388-6666)

Great Outdoors Trading Company, 219 Woodstock Avenue (US 4), Rutland, VT (802-775-9989)

Green Mountain Cyclery, 133 Strongs Avenue, Rutland, VT (802-775-0869)

Sports Peddler, 158 N. Main Street (US 7), Rutland, VT (802-775-0101)

9

South Royalton–Strafford

DIFFICULT TERRAIN; 27.7 MILES

With the exception of the Northeast Kingdom, 60 miles to the north, Orange County may be Vermont's most unspoiled region. It is a wonderland of wooded hills and winding river valleys. The county has no ski areas, large lakes, cities, or major mountains. Even Vermont's two interstate highways, 89 and 91, which enclose this unspoiled county on its south, east, and west sides, seem to funnel the traffic by, rather than draw it in.

This tour follows often-hilly roads as it crosses ridges between the First and West Branches of the White River. Carving a circle through the tiny villages of South Strafford, Strafford, and Tunbridge, the tour brings excellent views down the valleys and across the rounded hills whose streams feed the rivers below. Though the route is emphatically pastoral, the architecture is superb: three covered bridges, the outstanding Gothic Revival home of Senator Justin Morrill, and the exquisite village of Strafford, a cohesive unit of Greek Revival (1800–1840) residences and public buildings devoid of commerce and modern structures. If you make the tour in mid-September, you can also join the spirited whirl of the Tunbridge World's Fair. There are no restaurants after South Royalton, so it's best to carry food along.

DIRECTIONS FOR THE RIDE

0.0 Leave South Royalton by riding south on South Windsor Street, which runs along the village green, so that you pass the United Church of South Royalton on your left. Thereafter, do not turn onto any of the roads that intersect South

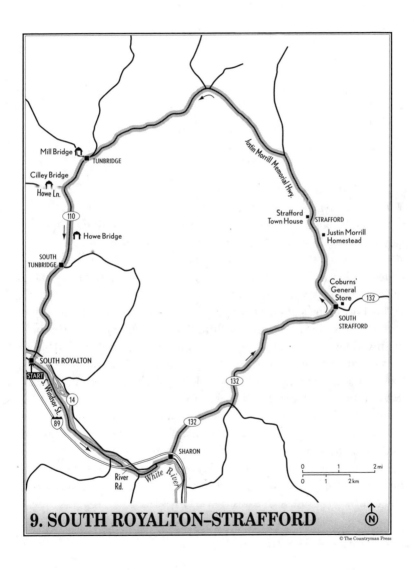

Mill Bridge

TUNBRIDGE

Cilley Bridge

Howe Ln.

110

Howe Bridge

SOUTH
TUNBRIDGE

Justin Morrill Memorial Hwy.

Strafford
Town House

STRAFFORD

Justin Morrill
Homestead

Coburns'
General
Store

132

SOUTH
STRAFFORD

SOUTH ROYALTON

START

S. Windsor St.

14

89

132

132

SHARON

River
Rd.

White River

0   1   2 mi
0   1   2 km

9. SOUTH ROYALTON–STRAFFORD

N

© The Countryman Press

Windsor Street. Just keep the White River on your left. At its end South Windsor Street becomes River Road.

Several small restaurants and a food co-op face the South Royalton green. A nice new and used book shop, Old Schoolhouse Books, is also there. On Thursday evenings during the summer the South Royalton Band performs on the green. South Windsor Street parallels the White River, which along this stretch offers spots to swim and fish for brown and rainbow trout.

South Royalton is the home of Vermont Law School, founded in 1972. The state's first and only law school, it is a private, independent institution that enrolls more than six hundred men and women from throughout the United States and several other nations.

The law school offers a traditional Juris Doctor (J.D.) that emphasizes the public-serving role of lawyers, a Master of Studies in Environmental Law (M.S.E.L.), and a post-J.D. degree, the LL.M. in Environmental Law. The school is also home to the Environmental Law Center and the South Royalton Legal Clinic. As the law school states, its character is rooted in Vermont: "Traditionally, Vermont's culture has been dominated by the village and small-town way of life. This culture has given rise to a strong set of values which are still prevalent here: emphasis on individual rights and responsibilities; concern for the community and one's neighbors; appreciation of a clean environment as well as a viable economy."

In Vermont aspiring lawyers can also gain admission to the Vermont bar by reading law with a practicing attorney and then taking the state bar examination.

4.7 At the stop sign and T—just after you cross the iron bridge above the White River—turn right onto VT 14 South, which is unsigned here.

5.1 In Sharon, turn left onto VT 132 East toward Strafford and South Strafford. *Within 0.2 mile, VT 132 tips steeply uphill for 1.5 miles, levels to a moderate grade for 1.4 miles, and then rises steeply again for a little more than a mile. It's a very challenging climb and the most difficult one of the tour. At the top, you start immediately down a glorious 2-mile descent. Initially the slope is extremely steep—13 degrees—so take it cautiously and enjoy the views.*

Joseph Smith, founder of the Church of Jesus Christ of Latter-Day Saints, also known as the Mormons, was born in 1805 on an outlying Sharon farm. He lived there until he was 10 and received his first visitation two years later in New York. About 5 miles from this intersection, at the end of a 2-mile climb up Cow Hill Road off VT 14, a quiet retreat has been built at Smith's birthplace. A monolith of Barre granite, 38½ feet high, weighing 39 tons—purportedly the world's largest—marks the site. Each foot of the obelisk represents a year in the life of the prophet, who was lynched by a mob at the Carthage, Illinois, jail in 1844. Had it not been for the organizational genius of another Vermonter, Brigham Young, born in Whitingham, Mormonism might have died with Smith.

7.4 Do not turn onto Bear Bridge Road (on your right). Go straight to continue on VT 132.

11.5 At the stop sign and T in South Strafford, turn left toward Strafford onto Justin Smith Morrill Highway, which is just a country road.

If you're hungry, get food here; it's your last chance. By turning right instead of left at the stop sign and riding 0.2 mile, you can buy groceries at Coburns' General Store on the left. Since the Justin Morrill homestead, a perfect spot to picnic, is just 2 miles away, consider carrying your lunch there.

In 2.1 miles on your right you reach the rosy pink, Romantic Gothic homestead of Justin S. Morrill, an extraordinary American. Take some time to stop here.

The principal building is a gorgeous example of a Gothic Revival cottage. Its elaborate Gothic shapes, normally cut from stone, are here rendered in wood. Finials crown the peaks of the steeply pitched gable roofs; bargeboards hang like icicles from the eaves. The interior is as fanciful as the exterior and includes novel solutions to contemporary problems such as airflow, heat, and protecting food from flies. Look closely—from both inside and outdoors—at the hand-painted screens, which cover the downstairs windows. From the inside you can see clearly through the screens, but from the outside you can see only their romantic depictions of European landscapes. None of the interior is visible.

Morrill designed this 17-room cottage, its outbuildings, and the landscaping. The cottage was built between 1848 and 1851. The entire homestead is now a National Historic Landmark and Vermont Historic Site open to the public 11–5 Wednesday through Sunday, Memorial Day through Columbus Day. Admission is charged.

Morrill was born in Strafford in 1810 and buried here in 1898. As the son of a blacksmith, he could not afford to attend college. Instead, he left school at 15 and made his way as a clerk and then the owner of several general stores. His financial success enabled him to retire in 1848 after just 17 years in local commerce. During the next six years, he built this home, studied the books he had been acquiring, married, and had the first of his two sons. In 1854 he was persuaded to run for U.S. Congress. Though he won his first election by just 59 votes, he was reelected to the House five times and then elected U.S. Senator six times. Morrill served 43 years under 11 presidents!

He is known best for the Morrill Acts, passed during the Civil War and in 1890. Both grew from his disappointment at not being able to afford college and from his vision that

Home of U.S. Senator Justin Morrill (1848) in Strafford

college must provide opportunities for "farmers, mechanics, and all those who must win their bread by labor," as well as those who enter the professions.

The Morrill Land Grant Act of 1862, signed into law by President Abraham Lincoln, granted each loyal state vast tracts of federal land for the support of colleges that would teach agriculture and the mechanic arts. Under this act and its successors, states received 17.4 million acres of land—nearly three times the area of Vermont—and 69 land-grant colleges were established. The Morrill Acts underwrote the first major practical and technical programs of study in American higher education, previously the exclusive bastion of classical studies in arts, sciences, and languages.

A quarter mile beyond the Morrill homestead, the magnificent Strafford Town House—some call it the Chartres of Vermont—stands on a rise at the far end of the village green. Local citizens paid for the construction of this splendid meetinghouse in 1799 by a subscription of pews and a special town tax levy. The Strafford Town House is not only the architectural center of the village; it is also the site of town meetings, weddings, concerts, and many other local events. One of the most interesting is the Strafford Town House Series. Sponsored by the Strafford Democrats, the series is designed to "provoke some critical thinking and discussions about current issues." Since its beginning in 1989, it has featured such nationally prominent speakers as John Kenneth Galbraith, Arthur Miller, William Sloane Coffin, Madeleine Kunin, and Tom Wicker. The series takes place Wednesday evenings in August.

13.7 As you approach the green in Strafford, bear right to continue on Justin Morrill Highway so you pass the green and Strafford Town House on your left. *Just beyond the green you start uphill. The grade is gradual but steady for the first 2 miles. It then increases to moderate for 1.3 miles and ends with a mile that's just plain steep. For most of the 4.3-mile climb, trees shade the road. At the top you get a panoramic view of the Green Mountains and have completed all the climbing on the tour. The road then drops steeply into a fast 4-mile run into Tunbridge, and the balance of the ride is easy.*

22.0 At the stop sign in Tunbridge, turn left onto VT 110 South. Make this turn very cautiously, for your visibility northward (to your right) is limited. *VT 110 slopes slightly downward as it follows the First Branch of the White River nearly the entire 5.4 miles to South Royalton.*

For more than a century Tunbridge has been celebrating the World's Fair of the Union Agricultural Society in mid-September. Sometimes drawing 15 thousand people a day, the four-day festival blends the exuberant spirit of a carnival with the exhibits and competitions of an agricultural fair. Folklore says that in years past all sober persons were herded off the grounds as undesirables by three in the afternoon. If you arrive during the fair, you can judge for yourself. For more information about the official events, call the Union Agricultural Society at 802-889-5555.

Within 0.1 mile after you turn onto VT 110, you can see the Mill Covered Bridge on your right. Built across the First Branch of the White River in 1883, its structure is multiple kingpost, with a span of 60 feet. A mile farther south, if you turn right off VT 110 onto Howe Lane, you can find the Lower, or Cilley, covered bridge. This bridge, also built in 1883, measures 65 feet. And finally, one mile farther on is the 60-foot Howe covered bridge (1879) on your left.

27.4 At the stop sign at the intersection, go straight across VT 14 onto Chelsea Street.

27.7 You enter South Royalton along the green, where you started.

Bicycle Repair Services

Biscuit Hill Bike & Outdoor Shop, US 4, West Woodstock, VT (802-457-3377)

Morris Brothers Mountain Bikes, 20 Bridge Street, White River Junction, VT (802-296-2331)

Omer and Bob's, 7 Allen Street, Hanover, NH (603-643-3525)

Woodstock Sports, 30 Central Street, Woodstock, VT (802-457-1568)

10

East Middlebury–Salisbury

EASY TERRAIN; 25 MILES (4.6 MILES UNPAVED)

This easy, lovely ride curves along the shores of Lake Dunmore, through open meadowland overlooking the Adirondack Mountains, and along shaded back roads, far from motorized traffic. It's a good ride for children as well as the rest of us. While it passes a very interesting old cemetery, a striking 19th-century mansion, a classic country inn, and several places to swim, it does not visit any towns of great note. On the other hand, the tour begins and ends just six miles from Middlebury, one of Vermont's most delightful villages to visit. There is a lot to do and see there. (See the Vergennes-Middlebury tour.)

My favorite times to ride this route are before July 4th and after Labor Day, since during the warm weather a substantial portion of the Middlebury population, as well as folk from other Vermont towns and farther away, move into "camps" along the shore of Lake Dunmore. The traffic still moves slowly in the summer, but there's definitely more of it. Try to plan to combine this bicycle ride with a hike to Silver Lake, as mentioned at mileage 15.0 below.

DIRECTIONS FOR THE RIDE

From the blinking red light in East Middlebury, ride south on Church Street. You immediately pass the front of the East Middlebury Methodist Church on your right.

0.1 At the stop sign, turn right onto Ossie Road (VT 116 South).

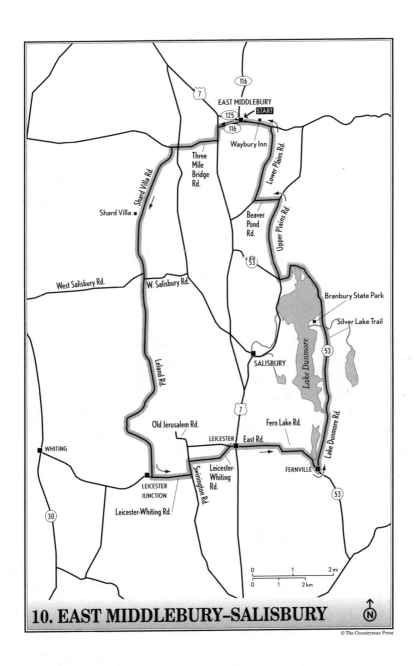

10. EAST MIDDLEBURY–SALISBURY

© The Countryman Press

0.6 At the stop sign, turn left onto US 7 South. Ride on the right shoulder of this busy highway.

0.8 Turn right onto Three Mile Bridge Road, which becomes Shard Villa Road within a half mile.

In 1.7 miles you get your first view of the Adirondacks on your right. In 1.3 miles more you pass the imposing Shard Villa Residential Care Home on your right.

The villa was built between 1872 and 1874 for Columbus Smith, a Vermont attorney who acquired a fortune by claiming European estates on behalf of American clients. Smith named it for Mary Francis Shard, on whose behalf he had successfully argued— over a 14-year period—an enormous estate out of the grasp of the English Crown. Currently, as Smith stipulated in his will, Shard Villa serves as a home for the elderly.

With its Italianate-Gothic-Second Empire hodgepodge of Victorian architecture and its on-site mausoleum, Shard Villa is surely the product of a man with a flair for the dramatic. The villa has three stories and 30 rooms full of frescoes and statuary. It is dark, somber, and imposing—an ideal setting for the many ghost stories it has spawned. Doors and windows mysteriously open and shut; household utensils vanish and then reappear elsewhere.

Peggy Rocque was no believer in ghosts until she moved into the villa with her devoted dog. But once there, the dog refused to follow Rocque up the stairs. It would stand rigidly at the bottom and just whine. Later, as Rocque lay in bed at night, she would hear glass shattering, but she never found anything broken. She also heard the piano being played but never found anyone at the keyboard. Once she discovered that the tub in an unused bathroom had been filled with water. This was especially odd because no one had ever been able to turn on the rusty faucet.

Jean Seeley, a former director, has claimed to have seen Columbus Smith walking the halls at night. And a housekeeper swore the old man's ghost appeared in his bedroom whenever she went in to clean.

Inside, the villa features local and exotic woods as well as wall murals by Italian artist Silvio Pezzoli. Robert Morris Copeland, an English landscape architect, designed the grounds, including the serpentine stone walls.

5.0 Go straight onto West Salisbury Road; do not turn right onto it.

Local records suggest that the first burials in the West Salisbury Cemetery (on your right at this intersection) occurred between 1795 and 1799. Twenty-seven Revolutionary War, ten War of 1812, and nineteen Civil War veterans are said to be buried here. See how many you can find.

5.1 Go straight onto Leland Road. Do not follow West Salisbury Road to the left, down the hill. In 1.5 miles, Leland Road changes its name to Old Jerusalem Road.

In 0.4 mile Leland Road/Old Jerusalem Road becomes unpaved for 3.3 miles. It is firmly packed and generally free of gravel. It rolls up and down three small hills over the next two miles. In three miles the Green Mountains come into view on your left, just as you pass Blue Ledge Farm, which makes fine goat cheeses. A quarter mile after the road becomes paved, you draw alongside Otter Creek on your right. It is Vermont's longest river, rising in southern Vermont near Danby and flowing northward 75 miles into Lake Champlain near Vergennes. The road becomes unpaved for the last 0.9 mile before the next turn.

10.3 At the stop sign and T, turn left onto Leicester-Whiting Road.

11.2 At the stop sign and T, turn left onto Swinington Hill Road toward Leicester.

11.5 Follow the main road, now again signed as Leicester-Whiting Road, as it curves 90 degrees to the right.

12.7 At the stop sign at Leicester, go straight across US 7 onto East Road, though it is not signed here. Walk across.

13.4 At the crossroad, go straight onto Fern Lake Road.

14.7 Continue straight on Fern Lake Road; do not turn onto Fernville Road.

15.0 At the stop sign, turn sharply left onto Lake Dunmore Road (VT 53 North).

In 3 miles you reach the parking lot on your right where the hiking trail to Falls of Lana and Silver Lake begins. It is a lovely 45-minute to hour walk to a wonderful secluded lake where you can swim and fish. Four-tenths of a mile beyond the trailhead is the entrance to Branbury State Park on your left, another great place to swim and picnic. The park's broad tree-shaded lawn reaches all the way to the clear waters of Lake Dunmore. Admission is charged.

A mile beyond Branbury State Park is Camp Keewaydin, one of America's most venerable boys' summer camps. Established in 1910, Keewaydin does not focus on the development of particular skills, as most contemporary camps do. It's a rough sort of place, where the motto is "Help the Other Fellow," and where campers spend five to seven days out of four weeks on remote hiking or canoeing trips. The nonprofit Keewaydin Foundation, which owns the camp, also runs a similar girl's camp, called Songadeewin, a bit farther south on Lake Dunmore.

20.3 Follow VT 53 North as it curves to the right.

20.4 At the crossroad, turn right onto Upper Plains Road.

22.4 At the stop sign, turn left onto Beaver Pond Road, which becomes unpaved in 0.1 mile for just 0.4 mile.

23.0 At the stop sign, turn right onto Lower Plains Road.

24.8 At the stop sign, turn left onto East Main Street (VT 125 West). You immediately pass the Waybury Inn on your right. Robert Frost often came here when he lived nearby in Ripton. The inn also served as the exterior set for the *Bob Newhart Show*. It is a delightful place to enjoy breakfast, dinner, or Sunday brunch.

The Middlebury River provides excellent swimming just 100 yards east—to your right—on East Main Street (VT 125 East) underneath the concrete bridge.

25.0 At the blinking red light, you're back in East Middlebury where you began.

Bicycle Repair Services

Alpine Shop, Merchants Row, Middlebury, VT (802-388-7547)

The Bike Center, 74 Main Street, Middlebury, VT (802-388-6666)

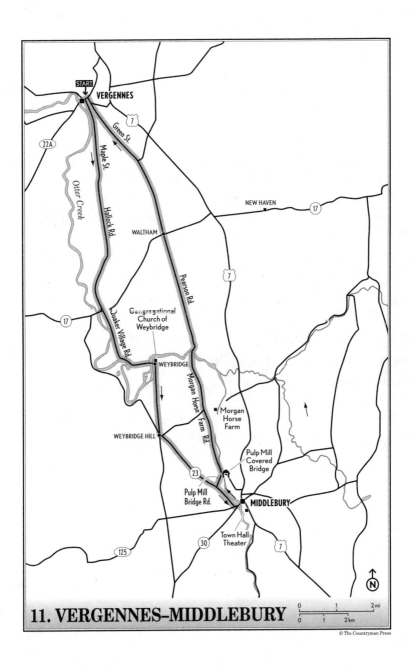

START

VERGENNES

22A

Green St.

7

Maple St.

Otter Creek

NEW HAVEN

17

Hallock Rd.

WALTHAM

7

Pearson Rd.

Congregational
Church of
Weybridge

Quaker Village Rd.

17

WEYBRIDGE

Morgan Horse Farm Rd.

Morgan
Horse
Farm

WEYBRIDGE HILL

Pulp Mill
Covered
Bridge

23

Pulp Mill
Bridge Rd.

MIDDLEBURY

125

30

Town Hall
Theater

7

N

0   1   2 mi
0   1   2 km

11. VERGENNES–MIDDLEBURY

© The Countryman Press

Vergennes–Middlebury

EASY-TO-MODERATE TERRAIN; 25.2 MILES

This relatively easy ride is nestled in the heart of the Champlain Valley, "Land of Milk and Honey." It explores fertile farmland overlooking New York's Adirondack Mountains and Vermont's Otter Creek. The creek created two delightful towns, Middlebury and Vergennes, each perched above a broad waterfall that accounts for much of the town's early prosperity and historic architecture. Each town boasts a wonderful variety of homes, churches, and commercial buildings, all of which grew from a vigorous 19th-century economy driven by the waterfalls. And each offers first-rate entertainment, so allow yourself at least a full day to enjoy both the bicycling and the many other attractions.

Middlebury is renowned as a college town and folk-art center and is far more cosmopolitan than its population of eight thousand suggests. It offers a pleasing variety of attractions that include the Vermont State Craft Center, the Vermont Folklife Center, the Sheldon Museum, several restaurants, nationally recognized inns, and lots of shopping. Often there are theater or concerts, outdoors or inside, at the Middlebury Town Hall Theater or the Center for the Arts at Middlebury College.

The citizens of Vergennes and neighboring towns have recently rejuvenated Vermont's smallest city (population three thousand). It now includes several excellent restaurants, nice shops, the recently refurbished Vergennes Opera House, and a marvelous array of classic architecture. Like Middlebury, Vergennes has a well-written walkers' guide that describes its most important architecture and tells you how to find it.

Vergennes Opera House and City Hall

DIRECTIONS FOR THE RIDE

0.0 The tour begins on Main Street (VT 22A) at the traffic light beside the town green in Vergennes. Ride just 1 block west on Main Street and then turn left onto Maple Street. As you make this turn, you will pass Eat Good Food restaurant on your left. It's an excellent place for breakfast or to order a fresh sandwich to take along.

In the winter of 1813–1814, Thomas MacDonough used the basin below the Vergennes waterfalls (a tenth of a mile farther west, down the hill on Main Street) to build three ships of Vermont lumber in 40 days! One was the 734-ton, 26-gun Saratoga. *Using these and nine refurbished gunboats, MacDonough saved Vermont from British occupation by defeating the British on September 11, 1814, in the battle of Plattsburgh. One of these gunboats, the 54-foot* Philadelphia, *used by Benedict Arnold, was later raised from the bottom of Lake Champlain and is now on display at the Smithsonian Institution. The cold, deep (up to 400 feet), fresh water of the lake makes a nearly perfect medium for the preservation of wood. You can see a replica of the* Philadelphia, *and other objects reflective of the lake's ten-thousand-year history, at the Lake Champlain Maritime Museum (802-475-2317) at the entrance to the Basin Harbor Club, 4.5 miles from here.*

0.1 At the stop sign, go straight to continue on Maple Street.

0.4 At the stop sign, again go straight to continue on Maple Street as it crosses Victory Street. In three and a half miles Maple Street becomes Hallock Road.

The terrain rolls gently up and down over the next five miles as you ride through some of Vermont's finest dairy country.

More milk is produced in the Champlain Valley than anywhere else in Vermont. Though Vermonters could once claim that the state had more dairy cows than people, it now has fewer than 148,000 cows—less than one for every four Vermonters. Nevertheless, that represents an enormous investment since the value of an average milker is about $1,700. Between 1977 and 2002, the number of cows being milked in Vermont dropped from 191,000 to 154,000, but the amount of milk produced rose nearly 29 percent because the annual output per cow jumped from 11,000 pounds to 17,500! During the same 25-year period, the price of raw milk, which is notoriously volatile as well as low, increased less than 19 percent: from $10.01 per 100 pounds to $11.89, and the number of dairy farms dropped from 3,531 to 1,512. In 2004 the price per hundredweight rose to $15.77. Vermonters also produce milk from goats, sheep, and water buffalo. Vermont *dairy farmers produce more than 70 percent of the state's agricultural income. The balance derives largely from other livestock, fruit, vegetables, and maple syrup.*

6.0 At the blinking light and stop sign, go straight across Otter Creek Highway (VT 17) onto Quaker Village Road. Be extremely cautious crossing this intersection; the visibility, especially to your left, is not good.

In a little more than 2.5 miles, you start gently uphill. After 1.5 miles of easy climbing, the hill becomes more difficult for the last 0.7 mile. As you ride along Quaker Village Road, you can occasionally see Otter Creek, Vermont's longest river at 75 miles. It runs northward from Mount Tabor, near Dorset, and empties into Lake Champlain just 8 miles west of Vergennes. Though pretty to look at and good for fishing and canoeing, Otter Creek is not an inviting place to swim. The clay along its shores and agricultural runoff give the water a brown hue.

10.0 At the stop sign, bear left onto VT 23 South (also Weybridge Road), and you will pass the Congregational Church of Weybridge on your left.

Before leaving Weybridge, indulge yourself with a half pint of the best chocolate milk anywhere. Just walk to your right across the intersection to Monument Farms. The James and Rooney families of Weybridge have owned and run Monument Farms since 1930. The Farms tend 350 Holsteins and process their milk weekdays at the plant here.

VT 23 goes gently up a hill for 0.7 mile. Along the way you get a nice view on your left of the Green Mountains, including Camels Hump (4,083 feet) and Mount Ellen (4,135 feet). As you approach Middlebury you will see McCardell Bicentennial Hall, the enormous science building at Middlebury College, on your right.

12.9 At the stop sign, turn left onto College Street (VT 125 East), though it is unsigned here.

In 0.1 mile, the Otter Creek Bakery is on your left. It makes delicious sandwiches and pastries, and you can eat outdoors at picnic tables. There are many other good eateries in this village. I am especially fond of the Storm Café. Other good, convenient restaurants are Mister Ups and Tully & Marie's. At each of them you can eat indoors or outside, overlooking Otter Creek. Another nice place is the Blue Hen, on College Street, just west of Otter Creek Bakery. It specializes in wood-fired pizza and delicatessen foods.

Middlebury has been a town of significance for two centuries. To gain a sense of its history and see what it has left behind, go to the Vermont Book Shop at 38 Main Street and buy A Walking History of Middlebury *by Glenn M. Andres. Then take a morning or afternoon to let this 80-page historical guide show you the village. As Andres writes in his introduction: "Middlebury has remained to a remarkable degree the village that the 18th and 19th centuries built.... Not merely of local historic interest ... [Middlebury's buildings] are of such range and quality that they can be taken as representative of almost every major style of American building from the colonial period onward." If you are lucky, you will be in town when there is a performance at the Town Hall Theater (802-388-1436) on Merchants Row.*

At some time during your visit to Middlebury, take a walk or a ride through the campus of Middlebury College, which begins on College Street, a quarter mile up the hill on VT 125 West. From rectangular Painter Hall, built of locally quarried gray stone in 1815 and now the oldest college building in Vermont, to the recently completed asymmetrical Center for the Arts, built of pink Tadaussac granite from Québec and designed by New York architects Hardy, Holzman, and Pfeiffer, the college architecture stimulates the eye. The campus is a New England hillside classic with broad views of the mountains and sweeping lawns, shaded by majestic trees of many species.

To learn what special events are happening, either stop by the box office at the arts center or call 802-443-6433. In July and August, you may hear little English spoken on campus. During those months, this liberal arts college of 2,300 women and men transforms itself into an academy of foreign languages, where all students agree to speak only the language they study.

After your visit to Middlebury, retrace your way along College Street (VT 125 West) to Weybridge Street.

13.2 Turn right onto Weybridge Street (VT 23 North).

14.0 Turn right onto Pulp Mill Bridge Road toward the Vermont Morgan Horse Farm.

14.3 At the stop sign, go straight onto Morgan Horse Farm Road, ride just 10 yards to the second stop sign, and there bear left to continue on Morgan Horse Farm Road, which becomes Pearson Road after you cross Otter Creek on the Rattlin' Bridge.

If you look to your right while you are at the first stop sign, you will see the Pulp Mill Covered Bridge. It is one of only two two-laned covered bridges in Vermont. The other is at the Shelburne Museum. There are only six of these bridges left in the entire country. This one spans 199 feet over Otter Creek and was built in approximately 1820 in the Burr Arch style. It is well worth walking through to take a closer look.

In another two miles you reach the University of Vermont Morgan Horse Farm on your right. Make sure to stop; it's a great place to explore, rest, or picnic. Admission is charged. The farm, a National Historic Site, is gathered about a great mansard-roofed barn, built in 1878 in the French Second Empire style. Information and guided tours are available there. About 85 registered Morgans are stabled at the farm, and some are usually out in the pastures or training ring. Several are national champions.

In 1795 a singing master, named Justin Morgan, brought a strikingly small colt named Figure from Massachusetts to Randolph, Vermont, to pay a debt. Morgan rented the 14-hand colt to a farmer who discovered that Figure had unusual stamina and quickness, a plucky disposition, and lots of style. Figure, who soon became known as "Justin Morgan," passed these fine qualities along to many sons and daughters and thereby began the development of North America's first breed of light horse. Morgan himself died in 1798, unaware of what his little Figure had begun.

Today Morgans are revered for their versatility and handsome appearance. They are trained for plowing, cutting cattle, dressage, jumping, pleasure riding, show, police work, driving carts, and trotting. During the Civil War, Morgans distinguished themselves in the First Vermont Cavalry. In fact, a Confederate soldier captured by the First Vermont was heard to protest that "it was your hawses that licked us." The Morgan is also Vermont's state animal.

Joseph Battell, a wealthy Middlebury resident, gave the Morgan Horse Farm to the United States in 1906. The University of Vermont now operates the farm. Battell loved Morgans and hated motor vehicles. In a slim book, he wrote presciently: "With what more lethal weapon can man be assaulted than the terrible and destructive motor car trespassing on the highway? Sooner or later it will come to this—the automobiles will be driven from the highways or the horses will be driven from the highways."

Three miles beyond the Morgan Horse Farm, you encounter a steep descent that leads you across Rattlin' Bridge. Keep an eye out for a sign saying STEEP HILL and get your speed under control. The surface of Rattlin' Bridge is made of wooden planks, which rattle loudly and can be slippery, especially when wet.

Just after you cross Rattlin' Bridge, the road changes name to Pearson Road and goes uphill for 0.6 mile. After the hill you have splendid views of the Adirondacks on your left.

20.9 At the stop sign, go straight across VT 17 onto Green Street. In three miles Green Street heads down a delightful one-mile hill.

24.8 At the stop sign, go straight to continue on Green Street.

25.0 At the yield sign, go straight across King Street to continue on Green Street toward VT 22A.

25.2 At the traffic light, you are back in the center of Vergennes, across from the town green.

Bicycle Repair Services

Alpine Shop, Merchants Row, Middlebury, VT (802-388-7547)

The Bike Center, 74 Main Street, Middlebury, VT (802-388-6666)

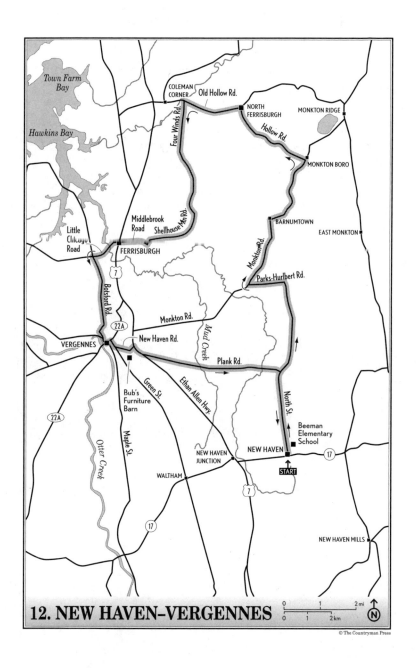

Town Farm
Bay

Hawkins Bay

COLEMAN
CORNER Old Hollow Rd.

NORTH
FERRISBURGH   MONKTON RIDGE

Four Winds Rd.   Hollow Rd.

MONKTON BORO

Middlebrook
Road
Shellhouse Mtn Rd.   BARNUMTOWN   EAST MONKTON

Little
Chicago
Road
FERRISBURGH

7   Monkton Rd.

Parks-Hurlbert Rd.

Botsford Rd.

22A

Monkton Rd.

New Haven Rd.   Mud Creek

VERGENNES   Plank Rd.

Green St.   Ethan Allen Hwy.   North St.

Bub's
Furniture
Barn

22A

Beeman
Elementary
School

Otter Creek

Maple St.

NEW HAVEN
JUNCTION   NEW HAVEN   17

WALTHAM   START

7

17   NEW HAVEN MILLS

12. NEW HAVEN–VERGENNES

0   1   2 mi

0   1   2 km

N

© The Countryman Press

New Haven–Vergennes

EASY TERRAIN; 30 MILES (3.5 MILES UNPAVED)

This is a splendid, easy ride with miles of fabulous views of Vermont's Green Mountains and New York's Adirondacks. The route adjoins thousands of acres of carefully tended farmland, and despite the fact that the local numbered roads attract lots of high-speed traffic, the roads you ride are nearly deserted. A little more than two-thirds of the way, you reach Vermont's first and smallest city, Vergennes (population three thousand), where you can eat very good food and follow a walking guide of the city's fine architecture. If you arrive on Memorial Day, you can see the state's largest parade. (For more information on Vergennes, see the Vergennes–Middlebury tour.)

The tour begins at the New Haven village green on VT 17. You can pick up a cold drink or sandwich at the Village Green Market on the west side of the green. The next place for food is Vergennes.

New Haven received its charter in 1761 from enterprising New Hampshire governor Benning Wentworth. Wentworth made a practice (and personal profit) of selling grants to land between Lake Champlain and the Connecticut River. The problem was that both the New York and New Hampshire colonies claimed ownership of this land.

Nine years later, on a visit to Portsmouth, New Hampshire, Ethan Allen purchased from Wentworth the governor's personal lot in New Haven, 500 acres beside the falls of the Otter Creek in what is now Vergennes. Such a purchase would be of little consequence today, but then it was one of many controversial land claims that actually drove history. Like many other land speculators of the time, Allen was prepared to purchase land even if it had a clouded title. The land he bought in New Haven was also claimed by a Yorker named John Reid, who had derived his title from New York's governor.

Allen was no faint-heart, and he asserted his claims with cunning and brashness. Nevertheless, when the American Revolution began, no resolution to the disputed land had emerged. So, in January 1777, when New York's attentions were elsewhere, rebellious landowners simply declared the region a nation of its own. This move legalized hundreds of Wentworth land grants and thus the economic interests of land speculators such as Ethan Allen and his brother Ira. New York, however, refused to recognize the fledgling nation of Vermont and continued to press its legal right to the land for 14 years. Only after Vermont paid New York $30,000 and agreed to join the Union as the 14th state in 1791 was the land dispute settled. Then the persevering Allens and other speculators got clear titles to what they'd bought from the enterprising New Hampshire governor.

DIRECTIONS FOR THE RIDE

0.0 From the New Haven green, walk north across VT 17 and begin riding on North Street. In 20 yards you pass Beeman Elementary School, formerly called Beeman Academy, on your right.

Most of the next two miles run slightly downhill.

Beeman opened in 1855, built entirely with funds from local citizens. Tuition paid for faculty salaries and other expenses. No enrollment figures exist for the school's first 10 years, but during the Civil War the academy fell on hard times. The townspeople began a fund drive to pay off the school's debt and create an endowment. Then in 1869 former New Haven resident Anson P. Beeman bequeathed the school $6,000 on condition that the trustees raise $4,000 more. Within a week the townspeople pledged more than $5,000, and Beeman Academy was reborn with a name that has endured.

The academy offered an "English course" to prepare its graduates for "the highest grade of teachers' certificates," a "scientific course" to ready graduates for "the agricultural and scientific departments of the best colleges in the country," and a "classical course" to enable graduates "to enter upon a full course of study in the best colleges."

By 1871 more than 60 students from 16 Vermont towns and 6 states attended the academy. As few as 20 percent of the graduates of the 1870s were New Haven residents; the other 80 percent were boarders. Gradually this ratio changed, and after 1900 the only out-of-town students came from nearby Vermont towns that lacked secondary schools. Now, Beeman educates only New Haven students in grades kindergarten through six. Approximately 160 students attend the school each year. Both my wife, Gail, and I have served on the Beeman school board, and our sons, Abe and Luke, have been students there. We sometimes wish our school budgets were as enthusiastically greeted, as was Beeman's 1869 challenge to raise $4,000!

North Street offers sweeping views east to the Green Mountains and west to the Adirondacks. It was once the grandest road in town and still boasts several striking 19th-century homes and barns.

2.2 At the stop sign, go straight across the intersection to continue on North Street. In 1.6 miles it becomes unpaved.

4.7 Turn left onto Parks-Hurlburt Road, which is unpaved. In a quarter mile it becomes paved for about 150 yards.

6.0 At the stop sign, turn right onto Monkton Road, which is paved.

In 2.7 miles, Monkton Road runs gently uphill for a mile.

9.7 At Monkton Boro, turn left onto Hollow Road toward North Ferrisburgh.

Over the next 2.3 miles, the road rolls gently down and up. When you reach the Monkton-Ferrisburgh line—three miles after you get onto Hollow Road—it changes name to Old Hollow Road. The road now turns dramatically downhill, and the Adirondacks rise above Lake Champlain to fill the western horizon. In a mile, as you head downhill, slow down to look for Four Winds Road on the left.

13.6 Turn left onto Four Winds Road. In a mile and a quarter, at the intersection with Dakin Road on the right, this road changes name to Shellhouse Mountain Road. In another half mile, Shellhouse Mountain Road becomes unpaved for a mile and a half. About a mile and a half after the road becomes paved again, look for a DANGEROUS INTERSECTION AHEAD sign and slow down for the approaching stop sign.

Along Four Winds and Shellhouse Mountain Roads there are more splendid views of the Adirondacks to the west and Vermont's Green Mountains to the east. Along the unpaved section of road, keep an eye out for the llama farm on the right.

18.5 At the stop sign, turn right onto Middlebrook Road, which may not be signed here.

19.3 At the stop sign, walk carefully across US 7 onto Little Chicago Road.

In 300 yards, you pass a large sand pile on your right. Scores of swallows often scoop nesting holes out of this sand. It's fun to watch them. In another 300 yards you cross a set of railroad tracks at an oblique angle. Walk across them.

20.2 Turn left onto Botsford Road, which is unsigned here.

If you would like to take a swim in Lake Champlain, turn right at this intersection onto Hawkins Road and ride three miles to Kingsland Bay State Park.

20.9 Bear right to continue on Botsford Road, which becomes Comfort Hill Road. Do not turn onto Tuppers Cross Road.

In a nine-tenths of a mile, just beyond three blue silos and a large, low, red-roofed barn on the left, the road points downhill and becomes steep. Keep your speed under control, for you are approaching the tiny city of Vergennes.

22.3 Go straight to continue on Comfort Hill Road; do not turn onto High Street.

The descent now gets steep, and you are fast approaching a stop sign.

New Haven dairy farm

22.5 At the stop sign, turn left onto MacDonough Drive, which is unsigned here.

You can get a glimpse of the falls on Otter Creek, straight in front of you through the trees. This is where Ethan Allen once owned 500 acres. MacDonough Drive goes steeply uphill to the next intersection. (For a story about shipbuilder Thomas MacDonough, see the Vergennes–Middlebury tour.)

22.7 At the stop sign and blinking light, turn left onto Main Street (VT 22A North).

Within 75 yards you reach Eat Good Food restaurant on your right and then the Vergennes green on your left. Eat Good Food is a favorite stopping place of mine and is popular with many cyclists. You can sit outdoors, eat inside, or get a superb sandwich to take to the green for a picnic. On the green there are benches, bicycle racks, a visitor information center, and a bandstand that makes a good shelter from rain or sun. There are several other restaurants in Vergennes, but there is no other place to purchase food later on in this ride. If you return to Vergennes for dinner, the Black Sheep Restaurant is delightful, and its food is delicious.

If you enjoy local history or 19th-century architecture, pick up a copy of Touring Vermont's Oldest City *at the information booth. This superb little booklet, which is free, will lead you on a self-guided and well-informed tour of Vermont's first city. The guide is divided into three sections, each with its own foldout map: History and Architecture, Nature and Recreation, and Cultural Resources. Within 2 blocks of the green there are many places to see, especially the restored Vergennes Opera House. If you're lucky, you will be there on the day of a musical, cinematic, or theatrical performance.*

22.8 At the traffic light (beside the green), turn right onto Green Street.

23.0 Just beyond the Vergennes Fire House on your right, follow the main road leftward. It is now called New Haven Road. In a tenth of a mile, you pass Bub's Furniture Barn on the right.

23.4 Follow New Haven Road around the leftward curve toward US 7.

23.6 At the stop sign, turn right onto US 7 South. Ride carefully uphill on the shoulder of the road; it is a main highway.

23.9 Walk very carefully left across US 7 and begin bicycling again on Plank Road so you pass the four-story, gray antiques barn on your right.

In four-tenths of a mile, as Plank Road starts gently downhill, you can see another sweeping view of the Green Mountains on your left. The highest peaks are Mount Ellen (4,083 feet) and, to its south, Mount Abraham (4,006 feet)

25.4 At the stop sign, walk across the railroad tracks and continue straight on Plank Road.

27.0 At the stop sign, continue straight on Plank Road.

27.8 Turn right onto North Street, which goes gently uphill for about two miles. You may recall that you rode this hill downward at the start of this tour.

30.0 You are at the intersection of North Street and VT 17, across the street from the New Haven green, where you began.

Bicycle Repair Services

Alpine Shop, Merchants Row, Middlebury, VT (802-388-7547)

The Bike Center, 74 Main Street, Middlebury, VT (802-388-6666)

13

Bristol–Hinesburg

MODERATE-TO-DIFFICULT TERRAIN; 36.7 MILES

This tour combines easy riding through farmlands with challenging terrain in the foothills of the Green Mountains. And it offers a delicious assortment of eating options.

Dairy farming—and Holstein cows in particular—dominates Vermont agriculture. But in Addison County farmers also produce apples, honey, maple syrup, wool, lamb, and beef. This ride passes many pleasingly small farms in valleys overlooked by the Green Mountains. Much of the ride also follows streams, known for trout fishing and swimming. From late July through mid-September, roadside stands overflow with delicious ripe vegetables.

The Champlain Valley was created during the Pleistocene glacial age. A huge sheet of ice crept southward from Labrador, rearranging rocks and soil, sculpting the mountains, and widening the valley. Waters from the melting ice and invading sea then flooded the valley to a depth of a hundred feet. Marine fossils are still being discovered here, well above the current sea level.

Bristol is a quiet, pretty, unpretentious village with one short commercial street. Consider starting your day with breakfast at Snap's or the Bristol Bakery, both on Main Street. After you complete the ride, you can have a good meal at Snap's; Cubber's Pizza; the Bobcat Café, which brews its own beer and often features musical entertainment; or sophisticated Mary's at Baldwin Creek, three and a half miles east of the village. While you're in town, stop at Deerleap Books at 25 Main Street; it's everything a country bookshop should be.

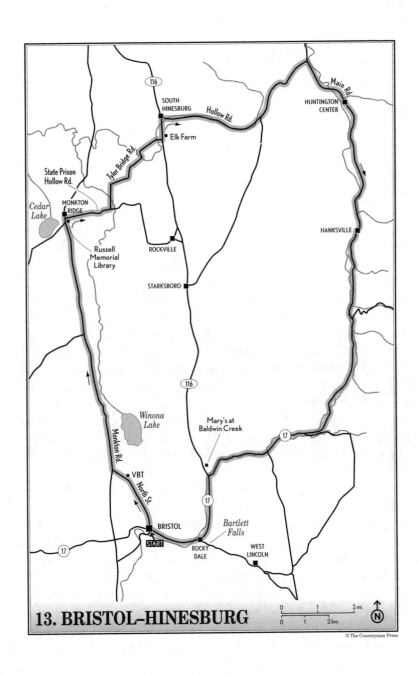

116

SOUTH
HINESBURG

Hollow Rd.

HUNTINGTON
CENTER

Main Rd.

Elk Farm

Tyler Bridge Rd.

State Prison
Hollow Rd.

Cedar
Lake

MONKTON
RIDGE

Russell
Memorial
Library

HANKSVILLE

ROCKVILLE

STARKSBORO

116

Winona
Lake

Mary's at
Baldwin Creek

17

Monkton Rd.

VBT

North St.

17

BRISTOL

Bartlett
Falls

17

START

ROCKY
DALE

WEST
LINCOLN

13. BRISTOL–HINESBURG

0   1   2 mi
0   1   2 km

N

© The Countryman Press

DIRECTIONS FOR THE RIDE

0.0 At the traffic light, on the southeast corner of the Bristol green, ride north on North Street so you pass the green on your left.

In a quarter mile you reach the creative country market, Almost Home, on your right. It makes excellent sandwiches and other take-out food. You might want to take food along for a picnic since the selection along the ride is not nearly as appealing as that in town.

In another mile and a quarter you pass the headquarters of VBT in a pale yellow barn and farmhouse (1848) on the right. VBT, known as Vermont Bicycle Touring when I founded it in 1972, is the oldest American firm offering country-inn bicycling vacations.

1.9 Follow the main road—from here northward known as Monkton Road—as it curves to the right. Thereafter, do not turn onto the side roads.

In 1.8 miles, by the Vermont Department of Fish and Wildlife Access Area sign on the right, an unpaved road leads to Winona Lake, which is a good spot to fish for northern pike and pan fish. Being shallow, Winona does not make a good place for swimming. A wide variety of Native American relics has been uncovered along its shores.

Three miles beyond the turnoff to the lake, Monkton Road tips slightly upward. The slope increases gradually for a mile and then suddenly turns steep for 0.4 mile.

8.8 At the intersection in Monkton Ridge, go straight and ride just 25 yards to the first road on your right. There, bear right toward Starksboro, ride 20 yards to the stop sign, and turn right onto State Prison Hollow Road, which goes downhill past the Russell Memorial Library, housed in a small clapboard building, on your right. The descent lasts nearly 1.5 miles until your next turn.

Before heading eastward toward Starksboro, consider riding northward 100 yards to en-joy the views of the Adirondacks sweeping across the western horizon on your left and the top of Camels Hump (elevation 4,083 feet) peeking over the Green Mountains on your right. You can buy a cold drink or snack at the Monkton General Store.

10.2 At the crossroad, turn left onto Tyler Bridge Road.

In about a mile the road turns nicely downhill for a mile.

13.0 At the stop sign, turn left onto VT 116 North.

You immediately pass an elk farm, surrounded by an unusually high chain link fence, on your right. You can often see some of the elk under the distant shade trees.

13.6 Turn right onto Hollow Road.

Fifty yards beyond this intersection—on the left side of VT 116—is the Hinesburg General Store, another place where you can get a cold drink and snack.

Almost immediately Hollow Road begins to go very gradually but steadily uphill for 4.5 miles.

18.6 At the stop sign, turn right onto Main Road, which is unsigned here, toward Huntington Center and Hanksville.

As you ride through this valley, you get splendid views of Camels Hump and several lower peaks of the Green Mountains to the east on your left. The terrain over the next seven miles, which parallel a stream most of the way, is easy to moderate. However, there are three real climbs of about a half mile each.

26.5 At the stop sign, turn right onto VT 17 West.

At this turn, the bottom or beginning of Appalachian Gap is immediately to your left. In Vermont, gap means a somewhat low spot among taller peaks. Gaps offer the best places to construct passes through mountains, but nevertheless they present major climbs and descents. From here to the top of Appalachian Gap lie two and a half miles of steep switchbacks. The top, where the Long Trail crosses the road, is 2,356 feet. On the other side of the gap are the "Ski It If You Can" Mad River Ski Area, the less intimidating Sugarbush, and the towns of Waitsfield and Warren. So ride to the top if you are seeking a serious challenge and very rapid descent.

Following the prescribed ride to the west and right, the terrain is easy for a half mile until you reach the final climb of the tour. It lasts two miles and has several false summits. Coming as it does near the end of the ride, it can be challenging. A mile beyond the true top, as you are heading rapidly downhill, the Jerusalem Corners Country Store is on the left. It's the last place for a snack before you reach Bristol. VT 17 then descends increasingly steeply and takes you through a series of winding switchbacks in the final one and a half miles. Ride them cautiously.

33.5 At the stop sign, turn left onto VT 116 South (also VT 17 West here), which will become Rocky Dale Road, East Street, and finally Main Street in Bristol village.

If you are ready for a splendid lunch or dinner, go to what Fodor's rightly calls "one of Vermont's gastronomic meccas," Mary's at Baldwin Creek. It is just a quarter mile to your right on VT 116 North. Chef Doug Mack and his wife, Linda Harmon, use fresh local ingredients in kaleidoscopically imaginative ways to create delicious, seasonally changing menus. The 1790 farmhouse that houses the restaurant also has four bed & breakfast rooms, lovely flower gardens, and walking paths that lead to the creek and into the woods. Reservations (802-453-2432) are recommended, though not necessary.

Whitewater kayaking on the New Haven River

In 1.5 miles, just before VT 116 crosses a bridge, a paved road on your left runs uphill to Lincoln and Warren. If you ride up that road a third of a mile, you can take a dip in a wonderful old-fashioned swimming hole. The New Haven River tumbles alongside the road through a series of playful cascades. The most popular place to swim is at the base of Bartlett Falls, at the top of the first rise. Irving Wesley Sr., whose 19-year-old son died while fighting a forest fire in British Columbia in 1943, gave the land surrounding the falls to Bristol in honor of his son. If you ride farther up, you can often find a pool all to yourself.

Continuing along VT 116, you reach the stolid Lord's Prayer Rock (1891) in a half mile on the left. Here, thanks to the generosity and righteousness of Joseph Greene—a Buffalo, New York, physician, who spent his boyhood in Bristol—the Lord's Prayer is chiseled into the face of an enormous boulder. Apparently, Greene thought the profane language of teamsters, urging their horses along Bristol's muddy roads a century ago, might be improved by this immense invocation. There's no evidence that the good doctor's efforts went unheeded, but, although the roads are now paved, the hillsides of Bristol still occasionally ring with the blasphemous exclamations of travelers.

36.7 At the traffic light, you are back at the Bristol green on Main Street.
If you feel like a treat, go the Bristol Creemee Stand, a quarter mile west of the village on VT 17. If you're in Bristol on a Wednesday evening between late May and early September, you can hear a free concert, performed by a citizens' band, in the cupola on the green.

Bicycle Repair Services

Alpine Shop, Merchants Row, Middlebury, VT (802-388-7547)

The Bike Center, 74 Main Street, Middlebury, VT (802-388-6666)

14

North Ferrisburgh–
Essex, New York

**EASY-TO-MODERATE TERRAIN; 31 MILES (4.2 MILES UNPAVED)
WITH OPTIONAL 5-MILE SIDE TRIP TO THE SHELBURNE MUSEUM;
OR 26.5 MILES (4.2 MILES UNPAVED)**

This splendid figure-eight ride features the sparkling waters of Lake Champlain, sweeping views of the Green Mountains and the Adirondacks, and two delightful half-hour ferry rides across Lake Champlain. Nearly all the cycling is easy, and every bit of it follows little-used roads. The New York portion of the route has a wild feeling about it—with long stretches of empty roads and few people. Along the way are two fine places to swim in Lake Champlain, two classic places for ice cream, and several places to eat.

Although a quarter of Vermont's 610,000 residents live within 25 miles of North Ferrisburgh, the route is bucolic and quiet. Essex, New York, is an ideal destination: tranquil, charming, pretty, and interesting—a perfect place for lunch, browsing, swimming, sailboat watching, or summer theater. The entire hamlet is a National Historic Site. The tour also offers a side trip to the extraordinary Shelburne Museum, one of the nation's great collections of American folk art.

DIRECTIONS FOR THE RIDE

0.0 From the North Ferrisburgh Post Office, at the intersection of US 7 and Stage Road, ride west on Stage Road so you pass the Mobil station on your right.

1.0 At the stop sign, turn right onto Greenbush Road.

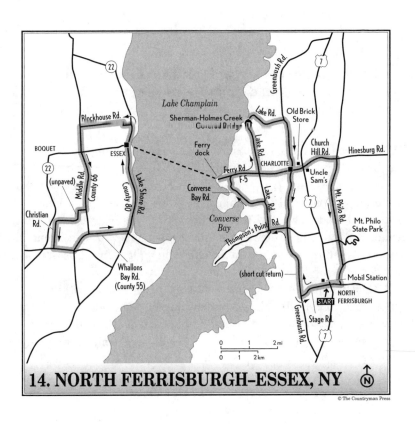

Lake Champlain

BOQUET

ESSEX

Christian Rd.

Middle Rd. (unpaved)

County 66

County 80

Lake Shore Rd.

Whallons Bay Rd. (County 55)

Blockhouse Rd.

Sherman-Holmes Creek Covered Bridge

Ferry dock

Ferry Rd.

F-5

Converse Bay Rd.

Converse Bay

Thompson's Point Rd.

Greenbush Rd.

Lake Rd.

Old Brick Store

Church Hill Rd.

Hinesburg Rd.

CHARLOTTE

Uncle Sam's

Mt. Philo Rd.

Mt. Philo State Park

(short cut return)

Mobil Station

NORTH FERRISBURGH

START

Stage Rd.

Greenbush Rd.

0   1   2 mi
0   1   2 km

14. NORTH FERRISBURGH–ESSEX, NY

3.3 At the stop sign, turn left and downhill onto Thompson's Point Road. In 150 yards you cross a set of railroad tracks.

Just before the railroad tracks, you pass a plaque on the right that commemorates the discovery of the Vermont state fossil. In 1849, in what had originally been the Champlain Sea, an 11,000-year-old fossil of a small beluga whale was found a little north of here about 9 feet below the surface. The 10-foot skeleton is now displayed at the Perkins Museum of Geology at the University of Vermont in Burlington. The museum is open 8–8 Monday through Friday and 9–5 Saturday and Sunday.

3.8 At the crossroad, turn right onto Lake Road, which becomes unpaved in 30 yards.

4.6 Just past the point where Lake Road becomes paved and just beyond a DANGEROUS INTERSECTION sign, turn left onto Converse Bay Road, which becomes unpaved in 10 yards.

Converse Bay Road runs gently downhill to Lake Champlain and affords lovely views of sailboats anchored in Converse Bay.

5.5 At the intersection with Cedar Beach Road—on the left and unpaved—go straight to continue on Converse Bay Road.

6.1 At the T and stop sign, turn left onto Ferry Road, which is paved but unsigned here.

6.2 You are at the ferry dock, where you catch the Lake Champlain Ferry to Essex, New York.

During most of the cycling season the ferry runs every half hour on the half hour. It takes 30 minutes to make the crossing. You can verify the schedule and fee by calling 802-425-2504.

6.3 After disembarking from the ferry in Essex, New York, walk to the stop sign and turn right toward Willsboro, New York, onto NY 22 North.

Allow yourself an hour or two to explore Essex now or when you return in 12.5 miles. In 1975 the entire pre–Civil War village was placed on the National Register of Historic Places.

Chartered in 1765 and then devastated during the American Revolution, the little town of Essex was one of the first European settlements on the western shore of Lake Champlain. During the first half of the 19th century, Lake Champlain became the primary shipping route between Canada and the American republic, and Essex turned into a magnet for energy and ambition. The Yorkers built a fine harbor to attract commerce, and their work was doubly rewarded when in 1823 the Champlain Canal connected the southern end of the Lake Champlain to the Hudson River and hence New York City. By 1850 Essex had become one of the largest towns on the lake.

This prosperity enabled some Essex citizens to build fine homes of stone, brick, and timber that still stand. Stop at the Essex Town Office to pick up a copy of the free pamphlet, Essex: An Architectural Guide. It lists 28 buildings of interest in the village and 18 more on the outskirts.

Just as transportation gave rise to Essex's prosperity, so it took it away. Shortly after the Civil War, the railroad tracks reached northeastern New York, and Lake Champlain lost its monopoly on shipping. Cargo began to move on tracks instead of water. Essex then converted itself into a late-19th-century summer resort for Bostonians and New Yorkers. But within 60 years travelers abandoned railroad trains for private passenger cars, and Essex was again passed by. It is now once more striving to capture the hearts of visitors.

6.9 Turn left onto Blockhouse Road so you pass St. Joseph's Catholic Church on your right. Blockhouse Road becomes unpaved in 50 yards.

Blockhouse Road is extremely hard-packed, with little loose material on its surface. It goes uphill ever so gradually and becomes paved in 1.3 miles.

8.6 At the stop sign, turn left onto Middle Road (Essex County 66).

9.4 At the stop sign, go straight to continue on Middle Road (Essex County 66), which is unsigned here.

11.2 Turn right onto Christian Road.

Christian Road goes uphill for 0.7 mile. Stop to look at the views behind you. Just as you reach the top of the hill and start down, Christian Road becomes unpaved and yields stunning views north and southward along the valley. The road becomes paved again after 0.6 mile. Keep your speed under control, because Christian Road makes a sudden 90-degree left turn just as the descent is ending.

13.3 At the yield sign and T, turn left onto Whallons Bay Road (Essex County 55), which is unsigned here.

Whallons Bay Road goes gently uphill.

14.0 At the intersection, follow Whallons Bay Road as it curves leftward.

Almost immediately, Whallons Bay Road starts downward toward Lake Champlain, affording superb views of Camels Hump and Mount Mansfield in Vermont.

Just before your next turn, you also get a great view of Split Rock on the far shore of Whallons Bay. Split Rock, which Native Americans called Roche Regio, marked the boundary between the nations of the Iroquois and the Algonquins. Later, the Treaty of Utrecht (1713-1714) established the rock as the dividing point between the English and French dominions.

14.6 At the intersection with Middle Road on your left, continue straight on Whallons Bay Road.

The descent really gets rollicking from here to the lake.

15.0 At the yield sign and T, turn left onto Lake Shore Road (Essex County 80), which becomes Main Street when it reaches the village of Essex.

If you'd like to take a swim, in 2.6 miles, just before you reach the blinking light in Essex, turn right onto Beggs Street and ride 0.1 mile to the Essex town dock. There is a small sandy beach there, and the water is crystal clear.

Camels Hump as seen from the west

18.7 At the traffic light in Essex, continue straight onto Main Street (NY 22 North).

Essex has several art galleries, antiques shops, restaurants, and a delightful ice cream shop. You can get more information about them at the Essex Inn or the Essex Town Office, both on the north side of Main Street. Also consider stopping at the Essex Theater Company (518-643-0888) on your right 15 yards before the entrance to the ferry landing to see whether it is presenting a play that interests you.

18.8 Turn right onto the ferry landing for your return trip to Vermont. It takes a half hour.

18.9 After disembarking from the ferry, follow the signs for Ferry Road (VT F-5). *The first half mile is uphill.*

20.3 Turn left onto Lake Road.

In 1.7 miles you cross the little Leonard Sherman–Holmes Creek covered bridge. It's just one lane wide, built in the tied arch style, and 39 feet long. Just beyond the bridge is the Charlotte Town Beach, where you can picnic and take a swim in Lake Champlain.

26.5-MILE RIDE (Though only 4.5 miles shorter than the full tour, this shortcut avoids about 2 miles of climbing and as much descent.)

Do not turn left onto Lake Road. Instead continue straight on VT F-5 and ride 1.1 miles to the blinking light—the last 0.5 mile is uphill. At the blinking light, turn right onto Greenbush Road and ride 1.9 miles.

If you're hungry, you can get a good sandwich or snack before turning onto Greenbush Road at the Old Brick Store, which is on your left at this intersection.

A mile and a quarter down Greenbush Road, you reach Pelkey's Blueberries on your right. August is blueberry season. The berries are excellent and well worth the stop. Pelkey's also makes good wine, which you can taste and purchase at the farm.

Six-tenths of a mile beyond Pelkey's, as you're going downhill, you reach an intersection where the main road seems to curve rightward. Actually the road that goes rightward is Thompson's Point Road, which you do not want. Instead, turn cautiously left and then immediately keep to the right to continue on Greenbush Road. (If you miss this turn, you reach a set of railroad tracks on Thompson's Point Road in a quarter mile.)

Follow Greenbush Road 2.2 miles more, which you rode in the opposite direction at the beginning of the tour. Then, turn left onto Stage Road and follow it 1 mile back to North Ferrisburgh, where you began.

23.5 At the stop sign, turn right onto Greenbush Road.

In 0.2 mile, you ride beneath a railroad trestle and go uphill for 0.5 mile.

SIDE TRIP TO SHELBURNE MUSEUM: If you can spare at least a couple of hours, cycle north on Greenbush Road to the Shelburne Museum. It's just 2.5 good cycling miles away.

Instead of turning right onto Greenbush Road, turn left and ride 2.4 miles to the traffic light. There walk your bicycle 0.1 mile along the shoulder of US 7 to the entrance to the museum on your left.

Nowhere in Vermont and few places in the United States display a finer or more varied collection of Americana. Both children and adults will enjoy themselves immensely. Founded in 1947 by Electra Havemeyer Webb, the Shelburne Museum consists of 37 buildings plus the SS Ticonderoga, the last vertical-beam passenger and freight sidewheeler remaining intact in this country. Spread over 45 beautifully groomed acres, the museum is open daily 10–5 from late May to late October. Admission is charged.

The museum reflects the eclectic taste of its founder, who began collecting American craft and folk art before its artistic merit was widely recognized. Among many other items, the museum contains railroad memorabilia, sculptured folk art such as cigar-store figures and waterfowl decoys, Audubon prints, a 525-foot-long scale model of a circus parade, and two galleries of fine paintings.

25.1 At the stop sign and blinking light, turn left onto Ferry Road (VT F-5), though it is unsigned here.

If you're hungry for a good sandwich or snack, you can get one before turning onto Ferry Road at the Old Brick Store, which is on your left at this intersection.

25.4 At the traffic light, go straight and very carefully across US 7 onto Church Hill Road.

Church Hill Road goes sharply uphill for the first 0.5 mile and then gradually up for another 0.4 mile. At the top of the rise, there's a good view of Camels Hump (4,083 feet) on your right.

Before you start up the hill, you might enjoy ice cream or a creemee at Uncle Sam's, a classic 1950s drive-in near the southeast corner of US 7 and Ferry Road.

26.1 At the stop sign, turn right onto Hinesburg Road.

26.7 At the stop sign and blinking light, turn right onto Mt. Philo Road.

Mt. Philo Road climbs two hills, each three-quarters of a mile long, and then goes mostly downhill with one half-mile climb near the end. Along the way you have spectacular views of the ridges of the Green Mountains to the east and the Adirondacks to the west.

In 2.5 miles, you reach the entrance to Mt. Philo State Park on the left. It's a steep 1.25-mile ride or walk to the summit, and well worth the effort, for the views of the Adirondacks and the Lake Champlain shoreline where you've just ridden are spectacular. Try it.

30.7 At the stop sign at the T (in North Ferrisburgh), turn right onto Old Hollow Road.

31.0 At the stop sign, go carefully straight across US 7, and you are back in North Ferrisburgh where the tour began.

Bicycle Repair Services

Alpine Shop, 1184 Williston Road, South Burlington, VT (802-862-2714)

Earl's Cyclery and Fitness, 135 Main Street, Burlington, VT (802-862-4203)

North Star Sports, 100 Main Street, Burlington, VT (802-863-3832)

Ski Rack, 81 Main Street, Burlington, VT (802-658-3313)

15

Waitsfield–Warren

MODERATE-TO-DIFFICULT TERRAIN; 19 MILES (0.3 MILE UNPAVED)

The Waitsfield-Warren area, known as the Sugarbush or Mad River Valley, offers extraordinarily pretty cycling and an enormous assortment of other activities at the foot of one of the East's major ski mountains. *Sugarbush* is a generic term for a large stand of sugar maple trees, and the word derives from the time when sap was collected and boiled to make sugar, rather than syrup. That process, which takes place in March, is still called sugaring whether its product is sugar or syrup.

The Valley, as locals know it, and two of its three ski areas take their names from the stands of sugar maples on Lincoln Peak and the neighboring hills. Like many ski centers, the Valley offers a wide selection of outdoor activities. You can go soaring in a glider out of the Warren airport, horseback riding at any of several stables, hiking on challenging or easy trails, golfing at the Robert Trent Jones golf course, and swimming, kayaking, or canoeing on the Mad River. There's also tennis at many inns and hotels, polo to watch or try to learn, organized off-road mountain biking, summer concerts, theater, nightlife, and many arts, crafts, and antiques galleries. The restaurants, bakeries, and specialty food shops can satisfy the appetite of any hungry cyclist. Despite all these goings-on, the back roads of the Valley are neither crowded nor overdone.

The ride is gorgeous and bypasses most of VT 100, where traffic can be heavy. You visit two charming villages, each with its own covered bridge; are surrounded by panoramic mountain views; ride on several maple-shaded back roads at the base of Lincoln Peak; and have an

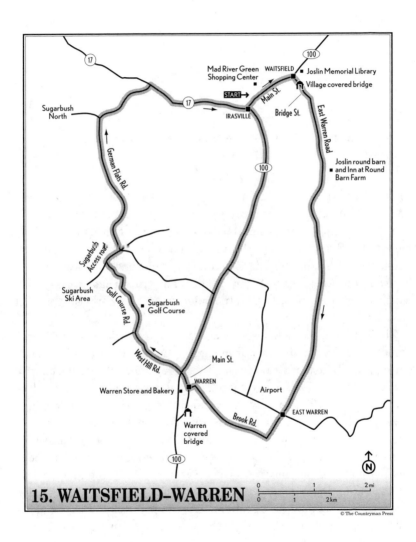

Mad River Green
Shopping Center

WAITSFIELD

Joslin Memorial Library

Village covered bridge

START →

Main St.

Bridge St.

East Warren Road

IRASVILLE

17

100

Sugarbush
North

German Flats Rd.

Joslin round barn
and Inn at Round
Barn Farm

Sugarbush
Access road

Sugarbush
Ski Area

Golf Course Rd.

Sugarbush
Golf Course

West Hill Rd.

Main St.

Airport

WARREN

Warren Store and Bakery

Brook Rd.

EAST WARREN

Warren
covered
bridge

100

N

0   1   2 mi

0   1   2 km

15. WAITSFIELD–WARREN

© The Countryman Press

opportunity to swim in the Mad River. The views are stupendous, the hills sometimes challenging, and the descents long and exhilarating.

If you want information about local events, pick up a copy of the latest *Sugarbush Area Guide*. Thanks to the hospitality of the Waitsfield Telecom Company, you can make free local phone calls from the blue public telephones set out for this purpose in the Waitsfield and Irasville shopping centers and the villages of Waitsfield and Warren.

DIRECTIONS FOR THE RIDE

0.0 Turn left out of the Mad River Green Shopping Center in Irasville—a half mile north of the intersection of VT 100 and VT 17—onto VT 100 North (Main Street). Walk across.

Before leaving the shopping center, you might stop at Green Mountain Coffee Roasters for some fine coffee, freshly made bread, pastry, cheese, delicatessen cold cuts, or other treats. You can also get a sandwich to go.

0.8 At the intersection—just *before* you would pass the Joslin Memorial Library (in a beige brick building on your right)—turn right onto Bridge Street so you pass the library on your left.

You come immediately to the Bridge Street Bakery on your right. It's a good place for pastries, fresh bread, and soups.

Twenty yards farther on, you cross the Village or Big Eddy covered bridge. Built in 1833 and recently restored by Milton Graton and Sons, the bridge reaches 113 feet over the Mad River. There's good swimming beneath the bridge. Just beyond it, East Warren Road begins an ascent that is nearly 3 miles long. The grade is steady but seldom very steep. It's the first of two trying climbs. Both are followed by terrific descents.

1.2 At the fork, continue straight uphill on East Warren Road.

In about a mile and a quarter, the handsome Joslin round barn rises on your left. Constructed in 1910, it is the last round barn left in the Mad River Valley and one of only a few still standing in Vermont. The barn is now the centerpiece of the Inn at Round Barn Farm. You then pass a series of lavish, white-fenced horse farms.

About 4.3 miles beyond the inn, East Warren Road tips downward into an increasingly exhilarating descent into Warren. Heed the road signs and ride the last half mile slowly.

7.3 At the crossroad, go straight onto Brook Road toward Warren Village.

The Joslin round barn (1910) in Waitsfield

Off to the west, on your right, the trails of Sugarbush Ski Area stand out clearly on the wooded slopes of Lincoln Peak (elevation 3,975 feet).

9.7 At the yield sign in Warren, turn right onto Main Street toward VT 100.

Before you make your turn, consider visiting the Warren Store and Bakery, which you reach by turning left onto Main Street and riding 30 yards. Located in a former stagecoach inn and library, the store stocks a delectable variety of foods and makes excellent sandwiches. Upstairs, a boutique sells clothing, fabrics, and decorative accessories. Next door are two arts and crafts galleries.

While you are at the store, get directions to The Arch, a natural stone bridge carved by the Mad River as it cuts through the rocky gorge. If you feel like stretching your legs with a short hike, ask the shopkeepers to point the way to the mile-long trail leading up Lincoln Brook. And before you leave Warren, stop to look at the Warren covered bridge that Walter Bagley built in 1880. The Mad River offers calm and clear swimming just above the waterfalls that flow below the bridge. It's less than 0.3 mile from the store to the bridge and swimming spot.

9.9 At the stop sign, go straight across VT 100 onto West Hill Road, which goes uphill.

10.1 At the fork, immediately beyond a bridge, bear left to continue on West Hill Road.

The next mile is tough, no doubt about it. But the payoff is great: quiet shaded roads, stunning views, and a terrific ride downhill.

11.0 At the T in front of the weathered sugarhouse, turn right onto Golf Course Road.

In 75 yards, the road becomes unpaved. The pavement resumes after 0.3 mile. Just as you reach that point, you reach the splendid, hilly Sugarbush Golf Course, designed by Robert Trent Jones. The slopes of the Sugarbush Ski Area dominate a panoramic view.

As you ride along the golf course, the road drops into a very steep and winding descent for 0.7 mile. Ride cautiously. From the bottom of the hill, there is one last climb—of just 0.5 mile.

12.6 At the stop sign, turn right onto Sugarbush Access Road, which is unsigned here.

12.9 Turn left toward Mount Ellen Base Area onto German Flats Road. The Sugarbush Inn will be on your right as you turn.

In 0.6 mile you start delightfully downhill for nearly 3 miles.

16.7 At the stop sign, turn right onto VT 17 East, which is unsigned here.

It's gently downhill for the next 1.7 miles.

18.6 At the stop sign, turn left onto VT 100 North. Walk your turn.

Over the next 0.3 mile, ride cautiously, for the traffic is heavy. A pleasing assortment of eateries, shops, and galleries line the sides of VT 100.

19.0 On your left is the entrance to the Mad River Green Shopping Center, where you began. Walk across.

Bicycle Repair Services

Fit Werx, 4312 Main Street (VT 100), Waitsfield, VT (802-496-7570)

Onion River Sports, 20 Langdon Street, Montpelier, VT (802-229-9409)

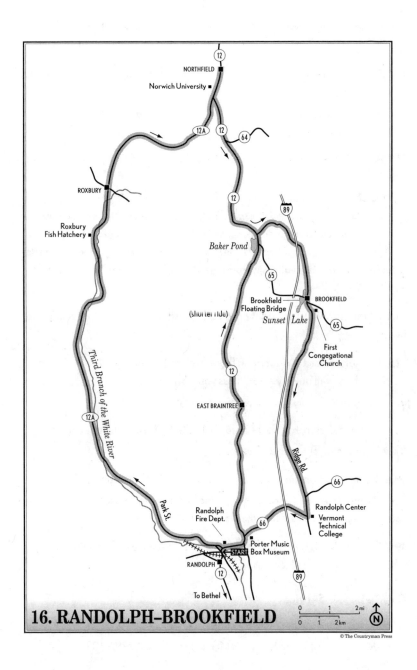

NORTHFIELD

Norwich University ■

12A   12   64

12

89

Baker Pond

ROXBURY

Roxbury
Fish Hatchery ■

65

Brookfield
Floating Bridge   ■ BROOKFIELD

(shorter ride)   *Sunset Lake*   65

First
Congegational
Church

12

Third Branch of the White River

EAST BRAINTREE ■

12A

Ridge Rd.

66

Randolph Center
■ Vermont
Technical
College

Park St.

Randolph
Fire Dept.

66

START   ■ Porter Music
Box Museum

RANDOLPH
12

89

To Bethel

0   1   2 mi
0   1   2 km

16. RANDOLPH-BROOKFIELD

© The Countryman Press

Randolph–Brookfield

MODERATE TERRAIN; 42 MILES (2.7 MILES UNPAVED)

MODERATE-TO-DIFFICULT TERRAIN; 26 MILES (2.7 MILES
UNPAVED)

A remote valley along the Third Branch of the White River, a floating
bridge over a sparkling swimming lake, an exquisite hillside village, and a rolling ridge overlooking the Green Mountains define this
tour. The landscape is a mixture of farmland, small lakes, woods, and
streams. On the fringe of the tour stand two small colleges, one a military academy, the other a technical school.

The longer ride is easier than the shorter because there is less climbing per mile, but both rides climb the identical amount of elevation. In
the shorter ride the climbing is concentrated in 10 rather than 25
miles. I find the shorter ride prettier and more interesting. It takes you
to lovely small farms and open fields at the beginning and then to a
shaded, winding climb through Brookfield Gulf at the end.

You are likely to enjoy these rides most if you bring your lunch
along. There is little available along the way, and Brookfield is a delightful place to picnic.

In 1975 Randolph witnessed the birth of Vermont Castings, one of
the world's leading manufacturers of cast-iron stoves for wood, coal,
natural gas, and propane. The company has its foundry in Randolph
and its assembly area 9 miles down the road in Bethel. Now employing
300–400 persons and annually producing 50,000 cast-iron stoves,
Vermont Castings is publicly "committed to a conservation ethic that
mandates the wise use of wood as a viable alternative to exhausting
the earth's energy reserves. A natural extension of this belief tells us

that a well-made, durable product, as opposed to one of short life, is another sensible way to save our natural resources." The stoves are beautiful as well as efficient. A showroom is in the center of Bethel at the Bethel Brick Store. It is open weekdays 9–5.

DIRECTIONS FOR THE RIDE

0.0 From the center of Randolph, follow VT 12 North (North Main Street).

On your way down North Main Street, you pass the Chandler Music Hall and Gallery on your right. Built in 1907 and well known for its fine acoustics and beautifully restored Victorian interior, Chandler hosts an eclectic variety of music, from Richie Havens to Italian opera. The gallery's exhibits change regularly and may include paintings, sculpture, photographs, or a special collection such as Vermont furniture or quilts. The gallery is open Saturday and Sunday 10–noon and by appointment by calling 802-728-9878. For information about events in the music hall, call the box office at 802-728-6464.

Randolph sits along the Third Branch of the White River at an altitude of 694 feet, the lowest point of the tour.

0.3 At the T facing the Randolph Fire Department, turn left onto VT 12A North (Park Street).

VT 12A makes easy-to-moderate cycling as it follows the Third Branch of the White River. Be very careful crossing the railroad tracks about 5 miles up the road. About 5.5 miles beyond the railroad-track crossing, you reach the Roxbury Fish Hatchery on your left. You can visit—and feed—the young trout being raised there to stock Vermont's streams.

26-MILE RIDE: At the T, do not turn left; instead turn right onto VT 12 North (Forest Street). Ride 0.1 mile to the stop sign, and there bear left to continue on VT 12 North, which you follow for 10.8 miles.

The first 7 miles are relatively easy and take you through a lovely valley of small farms. The next 3.5 miles are exceptionally beautiful, but challenging. You ride uphill through Brookfield Gulf, which resembles a winding crease in the side of a hill. Large, lush trees arch above the shaded road, and a little brook spills over its rocky bed. The gulf makes a wonderful contrast with the open meadows and panoramic views along other parts of the tour.

Three-tenths of a mile beyond the turn onto VT 65 (on your right) and immediately after you pass Baker Pond (on your left), turn right onto the unpaved and unsigned road.

Go 2.5 miles, and then resume following the directions below from mileage 29.2. (Do not use VT 65 to go to Brookfield; it is an unpleasant road for bicycling.)

The road is unpaved for 1.8 miles, but hard and smooth. The first 1.5 miles are uphill and shaded. Then the road becomes paved and runs parallel to I-89.

21.4 At the stop sign, turn sharply right onto VT 12 South.

If you would like to see the attractive campus of Norwich University or need food or drink, ride just 100 yards north on VT 12. Norwich University (1819) is a private, coeducational college, which serves approximately 1,900 cadets, traditional students, and commuters. It is the oldest private military academy in the United States; more than three hundred Norwich graduates fought in the Civil War. In 1867 the college moved from Norwich, Vermont, to its present location. The town of Northfield has a handsome common a mile farther north. The common is oval and surrounded by a striking white rail fence.

Northfield sits at an altitude of 760 feet, well below Brookfield at 1,481 feet, so a considerable challenge lies ahead. VT 12 goes gradually uphill for 5 miles before your next turn.

26.7 Turn left onto the unpaved road. Look carefully for this turn. If you miss it, you reach Baker Pond on your right in 0.2 mile and then VT 65 on your left. Though VT 65 does go to Brookfield, do not take it. It is an unpleasant road for bicycling.

The road is unpaved for 1.8 miles, but hard and smooth. The first 1.5 miles are uphill and shaded. Then the road becomes paved and runs parallel to I-89.

29.2 Curve to the left and follow the unpaved, unsigned road beneath I-89 and downhill.

29.5 At the yield sign, bear right onto the unsigned road, which is paved for just 0.1 mile and then resumes as unpaved.

The road goes gently downhill at first, and then becomes steep. Keep your speed down.

30.5 At the stop sign in Brookfield, bear left onto VT 65 East, which is not paved for 0.2 mile. The floating bridge and good swimming are 50 feet to your right.

The current floating bridge is actually the seventh such structure to span the 320 feet across Sunset Lake (also called Clinton Pond and Mirror Pond). The first was built in approximately 1820. That bridge and its successors were essentially rafts buoyed by empty wooden maple syrup, or later kerosene, barrels. When traffic crosses the bridge, it sinks slightly beneath the surface of the pond. The present bridge, constructed in 1978, floats on polyethylene barrels that are filled with polystyrene. Some people claim that a floating bridge is used here—and it is the only one in Vermont—because the pond is too deep to support a pillared span. Others claim that a tradition is a tradition, and Brookfield simply wouldn't be Brookfield if the bridge didn't float! In any case, the swimming and fishing off the bridge are excellent.

30.8 Just after VT 65 becomes paved again—beside the First Congregational Church on your left—bear right onto Ridge Road toward Brookfield Center.

For the next three miles, the road rolls up and down short, moderately steep hills. On your right, in the west, stand the Green Mountains. You can identify Killington (4,241 feet), Vermont's second tallest mountain, by the ski trails on it.

37.5 At the stop sign in Randolph Center, turn right onto VT 66 West, which is unsigned here.

Randolph Center is the original home of that especially American horse, the Morgan. Justin Morgan and his small, rough-coated colt, Figure, settled here in 1795. Now Vermont's state animal, the Morgan horse is extolled for the diversity of its abilities. It can

Brookfield floating bridge

be a cow horse, pleasure horse, equitation horse, or harness horse. The University of Vermont Morgan Horse Farm in Weybridge is on the Vergennes–Middlebury tour.

38.1 At the stop sign, turn right to continue on VT 66 West toward Randolph.

The next three miles descend rapidly back into Randolph.

Before you head down the hill, you might enjoy looking at the campus of Vermont Technical College, which is 100 yards directly in front of you. VTC, as it is locally known, is one of Vermont's five state colleges. It enrolls 1,200 men and women who are studying for associate and bachelor degrees in agriculture, business, engineering, and related fields.

40.7 At the blinking light, continue straight on VT 66 West.

In 0.1 mile you reach the Porter Music Box Museum and Shop, on your left. Walk across. It's an extraordinary place. You can learn about the manufacturing and history of music boxes. And you can see many exquisite boxes, musical automata, a 1926 Steinway Duo-Art Aeolian reproducing piano, and some of the unique Porter boxes made on the premises. The museum is open May through October, Monday through Saturday 9:30–5. From mid-August through mid-October, it is also open on Sunday noon–4. Admission is charged.

41.5 At the stop sign in Randolph, bear left onto VT 12 South.

Beware of the traffic at this intersection.

41.7 At the intersection beside the Randolph Fire Department on your right, turn left to continue on VT 12 South (North Main Street).

42.0 You are back in the center of Randolph where you began.

Bicycle Repair Services

Onion River Sports, 20 Langdon Street, Montpelier, VT (802-229-9409)

Peter Glenn of Vermont, 1400 US 302, Barre, VT (802-476-3175)

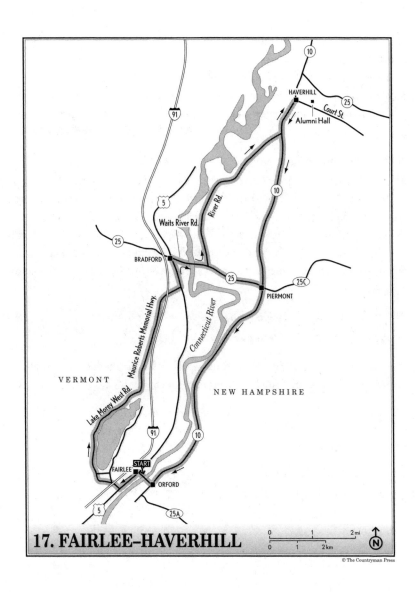

17. FAIRLEE–HAVERHILL

Fairlee–Haverhill, New Hampshire

EASY-TO-MODERATE TERRAIN; 24.1 OR 16.2 MILES

This tour explores a cycling paradise where Vermont and New Hampshire meet along the Connecticut River. The cycling is easy and the distances short, but make a day of it so you have all the time you need to explore what's along the way. Many of the attractions will appeal to children. There is a marvelous general store in Fairlee and an architectural scavenger hunt in Haverhill. Fairlee, Haverhill, and Orford are wonderful riverside towns, each in a different fashion. Fairlee has two intriguing antiques shops, an extraordinary general store, and a large lake. Haverhill is one of the most beautiful towns in the Connecticut River valley; its collection of federal houses and public buildings is nearly unrivaled. And Orford's dignified, multichimneyed estates are unique. Prosperous horse and dairy farms, glorious river views, extraordinary 18th- and 19th-century architecture, and lovely lakes sprinkle the countryside along the route.

For an extra treat, arrange to take a sunset hot-air-balloon ride with veteran pilot Brian Boland. It's a marvelous way to see where you have ridden. Brian operates seven days a week out of the nearby Post Mills Airport (802-333-9254). Also consider visiting Hanover to walk the campus of Dartmouth College (1769) and visit the shop of the League of New Hampshire Craftsmen at 13 Lebanon Street. It displays and sells works of more than two hundred craftspersons. Take your time along this tour; it will reward you well.

DIRECTIONS FOR THE RIDE

0.0 From the green in Fairlee, ride south on US 5 so you pass the green on your right.

Aficionados of road food as well as hungry bicyclists find themselves at home and well fed at the Fairlee Diner, less than a quarter mile north of the Fairlee green on the east side of US 5. It is a living artifact of the time when Americans traveled by road rather than super-highway and ate at local restaurants rather than international chains. And it's a great place to hear the latest local news. The diner is open daily 5:30 AM–2 PM.

Before leaving Fairlee, be sure to visit Chapman's General Store, at the northwest corner of the green. No ordinary general store, Chapman's displays thousands of hand-tied fishing flies, lots of stuffed fishing trophies, an enormous selection of wines, heaps of antique linens, and rows and rows of used books. See if you can find the moose head!

0.4 Turn right toward I-91.

0.6 At the crossroad—after you have ridden beneath I-91—go straight onto Lake Morey West Road, which follows the lake's western shore. Be sure the water is on your right.

The lake is named for Samuel Morey, who lived in Fairlee, Vermont, and Orford, New Hampshire, in the late 18th century. In 1826 he earned a patent for an internal combustion engine, and he may have designed and operated the world's first steamboat. In 1797, 10 years before Robert Fulton launched his Clermont, *Morey was plying the Connecticut River in a comical little craft, barely large enough to carry himself, a steam boiler, and an armful of wood. Morey showed his boat to Fulton, and some local boosters feel that Fulton, whom history honors as the inventor of the steamboat, received credit for Morey's invention. Morey went on to hitch an internal combustion engine to a little boat dubbed* Aunt Sally. *But he became discouraged and embittered by his repeated failures to convince the world of the usefulness of his inventions and ended up sinking his beloved* Aunt Sally *in Lake Morey. Attempts to locate the venerable boat have proved unsuccessful. Fishing for bass and perch is more promising.*

3.7 Turn left onto Maurice Roberts Memorial Highway.

This little country road at the northern tip of Lake Morey bears no resemblance to a modern highway. The first mile goes uphill, quite steeply at the end. Then, after a mile of easy riding, it goes uphill again for a half mile. From the top, the road shoots swiftly downhill for a mile—on sometimes-rough pavement—through three tight curves, the last of which takes you through an underpass. Ride cautiously.

7.0 At the stop sign, turn left onto US 5 North, which is unsigned here.

7.3 At the traffic light just south of Bradford, turn right onto Waits River Road (VT 25 South) toward Piermont, New Hampshire, and ride across the Connecticut River.

Just beyond the river, there's a short climb.

Bradford hosts a traditional country fair and a remarkable wild-game supper. The Connecticut Valley Fair takes place on the third weekend in July, at fairgrounds on US 5, just north of the village. Activities begin on Thursday evening and feature agricultural and homemaking competitions; horse, ox, and tractor pulls; carnival rides; and country-and-western music. Admission is charged.

The Bradford Wild Game Supper, which celebrated its 50th anniversary in 2005, is held at the United Church of Christ on Main Street on the Saturday before Thanksgiving. Parishioners prepare a gargantuan feast of rabbit, fresh and smoked wild boar, venison steak, bear roast, buffalo, moose, pheasant, beaver, and an annual surprise as well as salad, vegetables, and gingerbread with real whipped cream. There are five seatings, beginning at 2:30 PM. The supper is so enormously popular that reservations are necessary. For further information call Barbara Green at 802-222-4670.

8.2 Turn left onto River Road.

Heading northward on River Road, the cycling is easy until the last mile, which climbs a moderate hill.

FOR THE 16.2-MILE RIDE Do not turn onto River Road. Instead continue straight on NH 25 East for 1.9 miles more, about half of which goes uphill. Then, at the blinking light (in Piermont), turn right onto NH 10 South and ride 6.1 miles to Orford. From there, continue from mileage 23.7 below.

12.1 At the stop sign, turn left onto NH 10 North, which is unsigned here.

13.1 The Haverhill common is on your right, and you have reached the northern-most point of the tour. To complete the ride, turn around and head south on NH 10. The rest of the ride is easy and often downhill.

Before you go, look around this handsome village. Haverhill is a National Historic District and one of the most beautiful villages in the Granite State. Exquisite federal homes and public buildings face a broad, fenced common. The best place to start is Alumni Hall, two blocks east of NH 10 at 75 Court Street, which runs between the two halves of the common. Alumni Hall served as the Grafton County Courthouse from 1846 to 1891 and

some years later became the auditorium and gymnasium for Haverhill Academy, the local public school. Alumni Hall is now a community center dedicated to the preservation of
the cultural heritage and natural resources of the region and to the presentation of fine
and performing arts. There, under its beautiful arched windows, you can obtain information about the town and local events. Be sure to get yourself a free copy of Haverhill
Corner Quest, the whimsical walking guide and architectural scavenger hunt to the
village.

The enterprising New Hampshire colonial governor, Benning Wentworth, chartered
Haverhill in 1763. Wentworth made a reputation and nice profit by also chartering towns
in the disputed territory between New Hampshire and New York. That territory is now

One of the seven Ridge Houses of Orford, New Hampshire

Vermont, and Wentworth's chutzpah played a part in creating it. (For more on Wentworth, see the New Haven–Vergennes tour.)

In 1814 the stagecoach line reached Haverhill. For the next 50 years, horse-drawn coaches pulled into Haverhill every day. The nine hundred travelers they would bring in a typical week brought vigor and prosperity to the little town.

By mid-century, when railroads began to supplant stagecoaches, the citizens of Haverhill chose to opt out. They persuaded the Boston, Concord, and Montreal Railroad to alter its plans and run the tracks to Woodsville rather than Haverhill. As a result, the fire-breathing iron horses turned Woodsville into the center for transportation and commerce, while Haverhill remained pristine.

23.7 In Orford, turn right onto NH 25A West toward Fairlee, Vermont.

In the early 19th century after visiting Orford, Washington Irving wrote: "In all my travels in this country and Europe, I have seen no village more beautiful." Orford is no longer the thriving village it was before the westward exodus of the 1840s, but it remains a striking village of outstanding architecture on a grand scale. The buildings that line Orford Street compose a district on the National Register of Historic Places. Most prominent are the seven so-called Ridge Houses. These fine homes stand behind deep lawns, which set them far back from road. They date from 1773 to 1839 and were designed by a Boston architect, probably Asher Benjamin, a colleague of Charles Bulfinch.

24.0 At the stop sign in Fairlee, turn left onto US 5 South.

24.1 You are back at the green, on your right, in Fairlee.

Bicycle Repair Services

Banagan's Cycling Company, 187 Mechanic Street, Lebanon, NH (617-448-5556)

Morris Brothers Mountain Bikes, 20 Bridge Street, White River Junction, VT (802-296-2331)

Omer's & Bob's, Allen Street, Hanover, NH (603-643-3525)

III. NORTHEAST
   KINGDOM

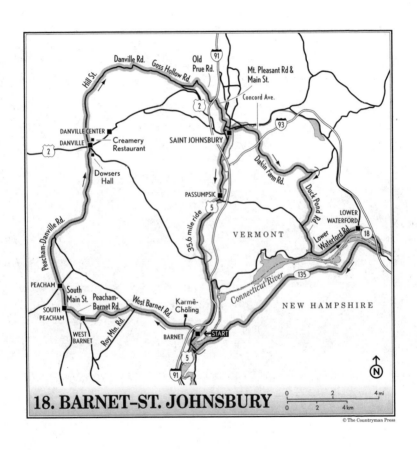

Danville Rd.
Goss Hollow Rd.
Old Prue Rd.
Hill St.
91
Mt. Pleasant Rd & Main St.
2
Concord Ave.
93
DANVILLE CENTER
DANVILLE
Creamery Restaurant
SAINT JOHNSBURY
2
Dowsers Hall
Dakin Farm Rd.
PASSUMPSIC
5
Duck Pond Rd.
LOWER WATERFORD
Peacham-Danville Rd.
35.6 mile ride
VERMONT
Lower Waterford Rd.
18
PEACHAM
South Main St.
Peacham-Barnet Rd.
West Barnet Rd.
Karmê-Chöling
Connecticut River
135
NEW HAMPSHIRE
SOUTH PEACHAM
WEST BARNET
Roy Mtn. Rd.
BARNET
START
5
91

N

18. BARNET–ST. JOHNSBURY

0   2   4 mi
0   2   4 km

© The Countryman Press

Barnet–St. Johnsbury

MODERATE-TO-DIFFICULT TERRAIN; 50.8 MILES (7.4 MILES UN-PAVED) OR 35.6 MILES (2.7 MILES UNPAVED)

From the tiny Connecticut River settlement of Barnet, this tour explores rolling countryside and tiny villages in what former U.S. senator George Aiken evocatively dubbed the Northeast Kingdom. It is the part of Vermont that has changed the least, the part many Vermonters call "the Vermonters' Vermont."

The first 13 miles bring challenge along with beauty as you leave the Connecticut River valley and ride westward into the hills of Caledonia County. The terrain is sometimes arduous, but the charm of the undulating countryside and the exquisite villages of Peacham and Danville make the effort abundantly worthwhile. At its midpoint the tour enters the glorious little 19th-century city of St. Johnsbury. The architecture of its brick commercial district, the outstanding public buildings, and the many fine Victorian homes is splendid. St. Johnsbury is home to a glorious public library and art gallery that feature one of Albert Bierstadt's greatest paintings and to a wonderful museum of natural history.

Both tours visit Peacham, Danville, and St. Johnsbury. The shorter ride avoids some climbing as well as 15 miles of riding. It finishes with an easy 10 miles along the Passumpsic River. The longer tour includes 7.4 miles of wonderfully smooth unpaved road, fine for either narrow- or fat-tired bicycles. The longer tour ends by crossing into New Hampshire for 10 easy miles along a ridge overlooking the Connecticut River.

DIRECTIONS FOR THE RIDE

0.0 From Barnet on US 5—with the Barnet Village Store on your left and the Barnet Post Office on your right—ride west and uphill on Monument Circle for 15 yards to the granite plaques honoring Barnet's war dead. There bear left onto Church Street. You cross a bridge and pass the 1854 Barnet Congregational Church on your right.

During the first week of October, Barnet joins Peacham and five other nearby towns in the Northeast Kingdom Annual Fall Foliage Festival. The celebration lasts a week. A different event—usually involving food, but sometimes also dancing, hiking, livestock, or crafts—is scheduled in each town daily. For details call the Barnet town clerk at 802-633-2256.

0.3 At the stop sign, turn right onto Bimson Drive toward West Barnet and Peacham. In 0.1 mile you pass beneath I-91. Thereafter, do not turn onto any of the side roads. Bimson Drive becomes West Barnet Road.

You immediately start a gentle climb as you begin to work your way out of the Connecticut River valley.

In a half mile you reach the driveway to Karmê-Chöling, a Buddhist meditation center, which sits 0.2 mile off the road on your right. Karmê-Chöling was founded in 1970 by a Tibetan Buddhist master and author, Vidyadhara Chögyam Trungpa Rinpoche. The center focuses on Buddhist and Shambhala teachings.

Architecturally, Karmê-Chöling is a vibrant juxtaposition of Vermont, Tibetan, and Japanese design. It sits on 540 acres of woodland, meadows, and ponds. The central building is a blend of farmhouse and shrine that features the first Kagyü shrine room in North America and a meditation hall for two hundred people. Guests are most welcome and can eat lunch or dinner there. But it's wise to call ahead (802-633-2384) to make sure no special event, which might preclude your visit, is going on.

3.1 Do not turn left onto Roy Mountain Road.

5.0 In West Barnet, follow the main road—actually called Main Street—so that you pass the Presbyterian Church of West Barnet on your left. Do not turn onto Stevenson, Garland Hill, or Old West Roads.

5.2 Just beyond the West Barnet Garage on your left, turn right onto West Main Street, which becomes Peacham-Barnet Road. Neither is signed here.

For the next 1.5 miles you head steadily uphill to South Peacham, which sits at 1,000 feet above sea level.

6.7 At the stop sign (in South Peacham), turn right onto South Main Street toward Peacham and Danville.

You now encounter the steepest climb of the tour. In barely a mile you climb more than 900 vertical feet to Peacham. Don't feel weak if you have to stop.

7.7 In Peacham continue straight on Bayley-Hazen Road, which becomes Peacham-Danville Road.

Don't leave Peacham without looking around. It's a Vermont treasure. The first thing I like to do is walk 50 yards up Church Street (which is unpaved and on your left) to listen to the silence, remarkable even in Vermont.

Peacham sparkles with white clapboard houses that were built more than 150 years ago. A few date from the 18th century. The village has something of an aristocratic air. Perhaps it derives from the fine architecture, perhaps from the retired professors, ambassadors, literati, and artistic luminaries who have moved there. The Historical House, an 1820s schoolhouse, is open July through early October on Sunday and Monday, 2–4.

The Peacham Store and the Peacham Corner Guild are both on your left when you reach Peacham. The store makes soup, chili, salads, unusual sandwiches, and coffee, including espresso and cappuccino. Try one of their homemade popsicles. The art guild, a cooperative, features the work of local crafters who take turns staffing the shop. Their wares include photography, children's clothing, quilting, and homemade foods.

From Peacham to Danville the cycling gets much easier. You descend nearly 600 feet over the next 6 miles. The terrain continues to roll but goes down more than up. In the late fall the hillsides turn yellow-orange thanks to the predominance of larch trees, also called tamaracks. This unusual genus of pine is deciduous; its green needles change color and fall off in autumn.

14.6 At the blinking light in Danville, go straight across US 2 onto Hill Street, which is unsigned here, toward North Danville. Thereafter, follow the main road, which becomes Danville Road; do not turn onto the side roads.

Danville sits on a plateau, commanding long views of New Hampshire's White Mountains. The village, its town hall, and large green are beautiful. You can get a snack at The Diamond Hill Store or eat a sit-down lunch at the Creamery Restaurant, on the right side of Hill Street, 35 yards after you cross US 2. The Creamery is open Tuesday through Saturday and features homemade soups, sandwiches, and salads. In 0.2 mile, Hill Street Park, which has picnic tables and shelter, is on your right.

In 0.7 mile Hill Street climbs uphill for 1.5 miles. It then turns downhill as you descend into St. Johnsbury. The first 1.7 miles of descent are moderate, the next mile is steep and fast, and the final 4 go downhill gently.

Thaddeus Stevens was born in Danville in 1792 and attended school in Peacham. A vigorous and outspoken opponent of slavery, he also fought Lincoln's plan for reconstructing the South after the Civil War because he considered the plan too lenient. Stevens represented part of Pennsylvania in the U.S. House of Representatives from 1849 to 1853 as a Whig, and from 1859 until his death in 1868 as a Republican. Leader of the Congressional Radical Republicans, Stevens broke with Andrew Johnson when Johnson vetoed a bill to protect the newly freed blacks from vengeful codes being legislated against them by many southern states. Stevens went on to lead the successful battle for the 14th Amendment and to conduct the House impeachment proceedings against Johnson.

Danville may be best known as the dowsing headquarters of the nation. The 5,000-member American Society of Dowsers is located here in Dowsers Hall, just a quarter mile down Brainerd Street.

Dowsing is a quest for information and is most commonly done by holding a forked stick or bent rod over the ground until the stick or rod moves to indicate a find. According to the society, anyone can do it, and almost all children younger than 16 are sensitive. In these days of complex electronic technology, dowsing seems nearly supernatural. According to the society, "Information comes to the dowser through a means other than the five senses." Dowsers frequently seek underground sources of water, but they also search for buried objects and even missing persons. A highly skilled dowser can stand at the edge of a field—or even over a map—and determine where water or some other object is located, how deep it is, and, in the case of water, how rapidly it is flowing. A good dowser can certainly unsettle the crustiest skeptic.

If you visit the society's headquarters at Dowsers Hall—open 9–5 weekdays—you can obtain some basic instruction and free literature. The annual dowsers convention, which met in Danville for 25 years, is now so large that it gathers instead at Lyndon State College in Lyndonville, Vermont. The four-day meeting usually takes pace in late June and includes more than 80 presentations. Call 802-684-3417 for details.

21.8 Turn left onto Goss Hollow Road. Ride just 20 yards across the bridge and turn right to continue on Goss Hollow Road.

22.1 At the fork, bear left onto Old Prue Road, which is unpaved and unsigned here.

22.7 At the T, turn right onto Mt. Pleasant Road, which is unpaved.

23.4 At the T, turn right to continue on Mt. Pleasant Road, which is still unpaved, but becomes paved in 1.4 miles. Do not turn onto the side roads.

Two-tenths of a mile after Mt. Pleasant Road becomes paved, you pass an unusual octagonal house at the edge of the residential district of St. Johnsbury.

25.2 At the stop sign, go straight onto Mt. Pleasant Street. Ride 30 yards to the yield sign and bear right to continue on Mt. Pleasant Street, which becomes Main Street and leads through the Main Street Historic District of St. Johnsbury. Do not turn onto the side streets.

In 0.3 mile, at 1302 Main Street, you reach the Fairbanks Museum and Planetarium—a Victorian whirlwind of towers, arches, limestone carvings, and red sandstone—on your left. It is probably the town's most elegant building. Lambert Packard designed it in the Richardsonian style. The interior, finely crafted of golden oak and cherry, rises into a 30-foot barrel-vaulted ceiling. The 160,000-piece collection, most of which is preserved in Victorian glass cases, is truly eclectic: Zulu war shields, Civil War artifacts, New England plants, Vermont geologic specimens, big cats, fish, snakes, mice, moose, bears, bats, and birds, including one of the world's largest collections of hummingbirds. Patron Franklin Fairbanks said at the museum's dedication in 1890: "I wish it to be the people's school . . . to teach the village the meaning of nature and religion."

The museum also contains Vermont's only public planetarium—it seats 50—and the Northern New England Weather Center, which provides the region with daily forecasts and meteorological education. In the basement, physical phenomena are cleverly presented by push-button displays that almost beg to be manipulated. The museum is open 9–5 Monday through Saturday and 1–5 Sunday. Admission is charged.

A tenth of a mile beyond the museum is the splendid St. Johnsbury Athenaeum at 1171 Main Street (on your right). The beauty and solace of this public library and art gallery make readers of the illiterate. The reading and reference rooms are intimate and comfortable; books are everywhere in reach; and the walnut and oak striped flooring as well as the paneling and furniture gleam with warm patinas.

The St. Johnsbury Athenaeum was named for Athena, goddess of wisdom and art, and was designed in the Second Empire style by New York architect John Davis Hatch III. It contains a 40,000-volume library and an art gallery lit by an enormous skylight, set in a domed ceiling. The gallery is the oldest American art gallery still preserved as it was when it was built—in 1873.

The gallery houses a permanent collection of nearly one hundred canvases, many from the Hudson River School. Included are works by Jasper Cropsey, Asher B. Durand,

James and William Hart, and Worthington Whittredge. But the pièce de résistance is Albert Bierstadt's 10-by-15-foot painting, Domes of the Yosemite. When it was acquired, the New York Times lamented that the painting "is now doomed to the obscurity of a Vermont town where it will astonish the natives." To that, Horace Fairbanks, who gave the Athenaeum to St. Johnsbury, replied, "The people who live in this obscurity are nevertheless quite capable of appreciating the dignity it lends to this small village."

Bierstadt was apparently not offended by the painting's location, for he returned often to view it and retouch it. In fact, at his request the Athenaeum constructed a balcony so visitors could view the canvas from a better vantage point than the floor. The Athenaeum is open without charge 10–5:30 Monday through Friday and 9:30–4 Saturday. Don't miss it!

25.7 Turn left onto US 2 East (Eastern Avenue), which goes downhill.

A round barn near the Passumpsic River

25.9 At the stop sign, turn left to continue on US 2 East, now Railroad Street.

FOR THE 35.6-MILE RIDE: Do not turn left onto US 2. Instead turn right onto US 5 South (Railroad Street) and follow US 5 South 9.7 miles to Barnet. US 5 follows the Passumpsic River, and the terrain is easy. When you get to Barnet, turn right onto Monument Circle, and you are back beside the Barnet Post Office, where you began.

St. Johnsbury sits at the confluence of the Passumpsic, Moose, and Sleepers Rivers. With a population of about 8,100, St. Johnsbury is the largest town in the Northeast Kingdom. Much of its history, architecture, and cultural life derive from the imagination and generosity of the family of Thaddeus Fairbanks (1796–1886), inventor of the platform scale and founder of the Fairbanks-Morse Scale Works. Many of the grand homes and public buildings along Main Street were built between 1830 and 1870, when the company's prosperity led to a tripling of the town's population. In the 1960s, when an out-of-state conglomerate acquired Fairbanks-Morse and threatened to close the St. Johnsbury scale works, local citizens raised money among themselves to subsidize the cost of a new manufacturing plant.

There are several very nice shops and restaurants along Railroad Street. The Boxcar & Caboose combines the pleasures of a bookshop and those of a coffee house. Northeast Kingdom Artisans Guild is a cooperative featuring handmade works in clay, fiber, wood, glass, and metal as well as paintings, prints, and candles of many Vermont artisans. Moose River Lake & Lodge Store displays a unique collection of rustic furniture, moose antlers, clothing, and camp blankets. And the American Society of Dowsers Bookstore sells books on dowsing and dowsing equipment. There is good food at Piccolo's Bistro and, one of my favorites, Elements, which is just 0.1 mile off Railroad Street at 98 Mill Street.

26.0 At the stop sign, turn right to continue on US 2 East across the Passumpsic River.

26.2 Turn right onto Caledonia Street, which goes uphill.

26.3 Turn left onto Lafayette Street, which heads uphill for 0.1 mile and then down for 0.3 mile.

26.7 At the stop sign, turn right onto Concord Avenue, which goes steeply uphill for 0.3 mile and then downhill through a residential district. Do not turn onto the side roads.

27.3 At the yield sign, bear right onto Higgins Hill Road, which becomes Daniels Farm Road in 0.5 mile.

Daniels Farm Road goes steeply uphill for 0.3 mile, continues moderately uphill for 0.4 mile, and then goes steeply uphill a second time for another 0.3 mile. It becomes unpaved at 29.1 and continues to be unpaved until 31.2. The road surface is excellent. From the top you descend almost continuously for 2.7 miles. Occasionally the grade gets steep, so ride cautiously.

31.2 At the stop sign, turn right onto Duck Pond Road, which is paved.

Duck Pond Road goes downhill for 1.3 miles and then becomes unpaved.

34.0 At the Y, bear left to continue on Duck Pond Road, which is unpaved and unsigned here.

Duck Pond Road becomes paved in 1.1 miles and begins to go steeply downhill.

35.3 At the yield sign and T, turn left onto Lower Waterford Road, which is paved.

In a mile Lower Waterford Road goes gently downhill for 1.5 miles.

37.8 At the yield sign, turn right onto VT 18 South and ride across the Connecticut River into New Hampshire.

39.3 At the stop sign, turn right onto NH 135 South toward Monroe.

As you ride south along a rolling ridge overlooking the river, you can see Lower Waterford and Barnet rising out of the trees in Vermont. As you approach Barnet, most of the cycling is downhill. It is a fine way to complete your ride.

49.7 Turn right onto Barnet Road toward Barnet and US 5, and ride across the iron truss bridge above the Connecticut River into Vermont.

50.0 At the stop sign, turn right on US 5 North.

50.2 Do not turn left toward I-91; continue straight on US 5 North.

50.8 Turn left onto Monument Circle, and you are back beside the Barnet Post Office, where you began.

Bicycle Repair Services

East Burke Sports, 439 VT 114, East Burke, VT (802-626-3215)

Park Pedals, 3550 South Walden Road, Cabot, VT (802-563-2252)

Peter Glenn of Vermont, 452 Railroad Street, St. Johnsbury, VT (802-748-3433)

Village Sport Shop, 511 Broad Street (US 5), Lyndonville, VT (802-626-8448)

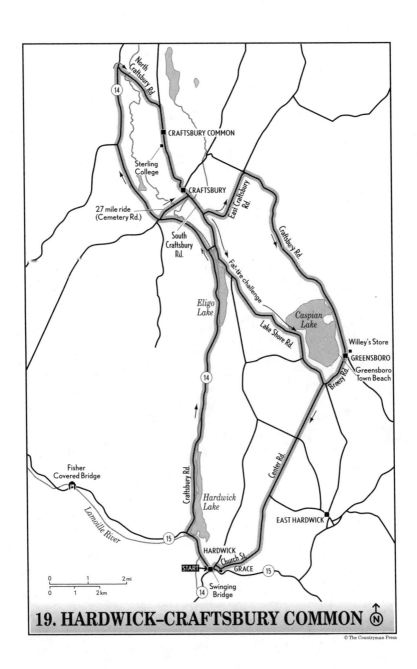

North Craftsbury Rd.

14

CRAFTSBURY COMMON

Sterling College

CRAFTSBURY

East Craftsbury Rd.

Craftsbury Rd.

27 mile ride (Cemetery Rd.)

South Craftsbury Rd.

Fat tire challenge

Eligo Lake

Caspian Lake

Lake Shore Rd.

Willey's Store

GREENSBORO

Greensboro Town Beach

14

Breezy Rd.

Fisher Covered Bridge

Craftsbury Rd.

Hardwick Lake

Center Rd.

Lamoille River

EAST HARDWICK

15

HARDWICK

Church St.

START

GRACE

15

14

Swinging Bridge

0   1   2 mi

0   1   2 km

19. HARDWICK–CRAFTSBURY COMMON

N

© The Countryman Press

Hardwick–Craftsbury Common

MODERATE-TO-DIFFICULT TERRAIN; 34.1 MILES

MODERATE TERRAIN; 27 MILES (0.9 MILE UNPAVED)

PLUS 6.4-MILE FAT TIRE CHALLENGE

Starting in Hardwick, this tour explores an extraordinary pocket of Vermont's Northeast Kingdom. Despite, or perhaps because of, its past as an economic backwater, this region of hilltop villages, glacial lakes, and conifer forests possesses a sort of pastoral magic. A bucolic stillness hangs over the landscape and is echoed in the laconic voices of old-time farmers and loggers. Even the jewel-like villages of Craftsbury Common and Greensboro, which have become expensive summer resorts, have lost none of their architectural authenticity. They are simple, handsome, and virtually unchanged by their new status.

So the magic persists: in Caspian Lake, in the nearly deserted roads winding their ways through the Craftsburys, and in Hardwick, where lives of hardship in the midst of beauty are so common. Few cars travel the roads of the Kingdom, although an occasional log truck does sweep by.

Spend a full day doing the tour, for few places offer more opportunities to meet a diversity of Vermonters than do Hardwick, Greensboro, and Craftsbury Common. And the Old Firehouse Gallery in Hardwick displays a collection of Vermont primitive art that should not be missed.

The 27-mile route avoids the climb into Craftsbury Common but unfortunately bypasses that stunning village. Enthusiastic mountain bicyclists who enjoy tiny roads and steep, steep climbs will love the 6.4-mile fat-tire challenge mentioned later in the ride. It adds a few miles to the longer route.

DIRECTIONS FOR THE RIDE

0.0 From the blinking light where South Main Street crosses VT 14 (Wolcott Street) in Hardwick, follow VT 14 North and VT 15 West.

If you approached Hardwick from the west, you may have noticed an unusual covered bridge on the south side of VT 15, about 4 miles west of Hardwick. The Fisher covered bridge, which extends 103 feet over the Lamoille River, was built in 1908 by the St. Johnsbury and Lamoille Railroad. It is the last railroad covered bridge still used in Vermont and one of only a few left in the country. A cupola, which runs the length of the bridge, serves as a vent for locomotive smoke and distinguishes this covered bridge from others. Scheduled for replacement in 1968, the bridge was saved by private donations and state funds, which paid to install supportive steel beams beneath its floor.

Although you can buy food in Craftsbury and Greensboro, the best selection for a picnic is in Hardwick at the Buffalo Mountain Co-op and its café on Main Street. The co-op also acts as a de facto community center for the many thoughtful, artistic, and politically active citizens who make this little town a vibrant hub for the Vermonters who live in the surrounding farm and forest lands. The co-op is the best place to find out what's going on nearby.

Diagonally across Main Street from the co-op, the Hardwick swinging bridge hangs above the Lamoille River. Be sure to walk across this tiny suspension bridge, which will ripple under the weight of your footsteps. The Lamoille River is merely a big stream here, because it rises just 8 miles away. But it becomes one of the four principal rivers in Vermont—the others being the Missisquoi, Winooski, and Otter Creek. They all flow into Lake Champlain, and all but Otter Creek apparently ran their present courses before the Green Mountains formed. They flowed so vigorously that they were able to maintain their westward movement despite the rising mountains.

Hardwick was a simple agricultural town until 1868, when Henry R. Mack discovered granite nearby. Then the area went through a dramatic transformation, becoming one of the granite centers of the nation. Like a booming mining town, it rode the crest of prosperity into a period of frenetic, haphazard growth that ended in the 1920s.

1.1 Turn right to continue on VT 14 North toward Newport.

VT 14 goes imperceptibly uphill. Hardwick Lake is immediately on your right; five miles later you pass Eligo Lake. The Black River, which flows into Lake Eligo, was called Eligosigo, which means "a good place to hunt" by Native American Abenakis.

8.2 Do not turn onto South Craftsbury Road; continue straight on VT 14 North.

FOR THE 27-MILE RIDE: Go only 8.7 miles on VT 14 North—or just 1.7 miles beyond South Craftsbury Road. Then turn right onto Cemetery Road, which is unpaved but smooth and hard. Follow Cemetery Road straight 0.9 mile—do not turn onto the side roads—to the stop sign. There, turn right onto South Craftsbury Road, ride 0.4 mile, and resume following the directions below from mileage 18.2. (If you want a snack, turn left at the stop sign and ride 0.2 mile into Craftsbury, where there are two general stores.)

11.9 Do not turn onto North Wolcott Road; continue straight on VT 14 North.

13.8 Turn right onto North Craftsbury Road.

In 0.3 mile, you begin the 2-mile climb up to Craftsbury Common. It is the most difficult climb of the tour, but at the top you find yourself in an ethereally beautiful village. Trim houses, uniformly gleaming with white clapboards and green shutters, proudly face a white-fenced green and bandstand. Beyond the houses there are commanding views across broad valleys to mountains in the east and west. Almost entirely free of commercial establishments, this picturesque village must be one of the most memorable in New England. Its dignified neatness accentuates the simplicity of line and color in its classic architecture. Giant sugar maples shade lawns set behind white picket fences, and the towering spire of the United Church of Craftsbury (1820) elegantly presides over the stillness.

Just beyond the green is Stardust Books and Café (on the left), a lovely place to pause for coffee and a look at a newspaper.

Craftsbury Common is also the home of Sterling College. Founded in 1958 as a boys' preparatory school, Sterling altered direction in the mid-1970s toward liberal studies, emphasizing outdoor challenge and nonacademic experience. Given higher-education status in 1978, Sterling began granting associate of arts degrees four years later and baccalaureate degrees in 1997. It now enrolls approximately 90 young women and men. Sterling College strives to "combine structured academic study with experiential challenges and plain hard work to build responsible problem solvers who become stewards of the environment." The hundred-plus-acre campus includes 12 buildings.

As you continue south out of Craftsbury Common, North Craftsbury Road becomes South Craftsbury Road, and you head steeply downhill for 0.7 mile. There are two general stores at the end of the descent in Craftsbury.

18.2 Turn left onto East Craftsbury Road, which goes steeply uphill for 0.5 mile and then modestly uphill for a mile more. Thereafter you climb gradually for three miles.

In 0.3 mile you reach Highland Lodge (on your left), which serves a nice sit-down lunch from noon until 2.

6.4-MILE FAT-TIRE CHALLENGE: Only the first 3.1 miles, where the grade is steep and the road surface rough, are challenging.

Do not turn onto East Craftsbury Road. Instead continue straight on South Craftsbury Road. Ride only 0.8 mile and turn left onto Lake Road, which is unpaved, and follow it 1 mile. Just as Eligo Lake comes into view on your right, Lake Road starts to climb, and the road surface begins to deteriorate. If the recent weather has been wet, the surface is probably soft and, in places, badly rutted. The road then narrows until it is barely 8 feet wide. It feels more like a hiking trail cut into a wooded hillside than a road. And it's monstrously steep.

Just beyond the first house you see (on your right), bear left onto Harrington Road, which is unsigned here, and follow it 1.1 miles. For the first quarter mile the road surface may be terrible, and the grade is very steep. Then the road surface improves somewhat, and in another 0.2 mile the grade becomes moderate.

At the T, turn left onto Lakeview Road, which is unpaved but wider and not as rough. Ride just 0.4 mile to the stop sign and crossroads. Lakeview Road goes uphill for 0.2 mile, and you get your first view of Caspian Lake.

At the stop sign and crossroads, turn right onto Lake Shore Road, which is unpaved and smooth. Ride 2.2 miles—do not turn onto the side roads—to the stop sign and crossroads. There turn left onto Breezy Road, which is paved, and ride 0.9 mile to Willey's Store (on your right). At Willey's Store, turn around and resume following the directions below from mileage 27.4.

25.3 Go straight to continue on Craftsbury Road, which is unsigned here. You will immediately pass the United Church of Christ (on your right).

27.4 At the intersection in Greensboro, beside Willey's Store (on your left), go straight onto Breezy Avenue so you pass Willey's on your left.

Greensboro is a rather exclusive summer retreat, favored by prosperous writers and intellectuals. Willey's Store serves as the meeting place for local citizens and summer visitors. At Willey's you can buy almost everything you need to be comfortable on the shores of Caspian Lake: dry flies to doorknobs; drum sticks to dish detergent; dry wine to daily newspapers. It's also a good place to buy food for a picnic.

Greensboro was sited here because Greensboro Brook, which tumbles out of Caspian Lake, was a good source of power. One gristmill formerly served by the brook is now a delightful shop, Miller's Thumb. Owners Rob and Anne Brigham import and sell Italian and Tunisian ceramics as well as an attractive assortment of locally made pottery, paintings, antiques, and furniture. Their building was constructed in the 1850s. When you go in, be sure to look at Greensboro Brook through the glass-covered opening in the floor.

The grassy Greensboro town beach is a fine place to picnic and swim. Just turn right beside Miller's Thumb onto Beach Road and ride 0.2 mile. Surrounded by low hills and wooded shores, Caspian Lake is one of Vermont's most beautiful and undisturbed lakes. Its crystalline waters are fed by springs and offer splendid swimming and fishing. Summer residents check the water's purity three times a week.

28.3 At the crossroads, go straight onto Center Road, which in 5 miles (in Hardwick) becomes Church Street. Do not turn onto the side roads.

Center Road rolls up and down for the next 5 miles. Several of the descents are steep and fast. Since Greensboro sits at an elevation of 1,463 feet, 800 feet above Hardwick, you go downhill more than up.

33.9 At the blinking light and stop sign, turn left onto North Main Street.

Caspian Lake, Greensboro

34.0 At the stop sign, turn right onto VT 15 West.

34.1 You are back where you began, at the blinking light where South Main Street crosses VT 14 (Wolcott Street).

While you're still in Hardwick, don't fail to visit GRACE (Vermont's Grass Roots Art and Community Effort) at the Old Firehouse, diagonally across Mill Street from the post office.

GRACE is a nonprofit organization that, through instruction, encouragement, and workspace, enables adults and children to develop the artists within themselves. You will find individuals at work, walls teeming with art, and bins of finished paintings to see and buy. GRACE is open by appointment (call 802-472-6857) and 10–4 Tuesday through Thursday.

Barbara R. Luck, curator of the Abby Aldrich Rockefeller Folk Art Center in Williamsburg, Virginia, wrote: "GRACE artists can hold their own among Madison Avenue's best. Illustrating originality and inventiveness in their subject interpretations and in their handling of form, line, and color, works produced by GRACE artists quite often exhibit extraordinary aesthetic quality and appeal, and they may be judged entirely on their own merits." Gayleen Aiken, renowned Barre, Vermont, "artist, film star, camper, comic cartoonist, and musician" (her tongue-in-cheek self-description) left GRACE most of her unsold work. It is stored and exhibited here. Some of it is for sale. Like many GRACE artists, Aiken lacked formal training, took many of her scenes from a challenging life in Vermont, and used words as well as vivid color to bring her fantastic images to life.

Two doors down from GRACE is Linda Ramsdell's splendid Galaxy Bookshop, which has a wide selection of books by Vermont authors as well as contemporary and classic works.

Bicycle Repair Services

Chuck's Bikes, Main Street, Morrisville, VT (802-888-7642)

Onion River Sports, 20 Langdon Street, Montpelier, VT (802-229-8409)

Park Pedals, 3550 South Walden Road, Cabot, VT (802-563-2252)

Peter Glenn of Vermont, 1400 US 302, Barre, VT (802-476-3175)

20

Lyndonville–Barton

EASY-TO-MODERATE TERRAIN; 49.7 MILES

Vermont's northern piedmont and glaciated Connecticut River highlands have been known as the Northeast Kingdom since former U.S. senator George Aiken so dubbed them in 1949. This region, the poorest and most sparsely settled of the state, retains an ethereal quality, difficult to define, yet evident to those who take the time to explore it.

This half-century ride follows generally easy terrain to the deep glacial lakes, conifer forests, and tiny villages for which the Kingdom is renowned. You can swim in Lake Willoughby and Crystal Lake; enjoy ice cream treats at antique soda fountains in Lyndonville and Barton; and rummage through the Bread and Puppet Theater's old barn of a museum. Along the way, you encounter very little traffic, ride through a covered bridge, and see one splendid view after another. For me the Northeast Kingdom—in temperament and appearance—is the Vermonter's Vermont. This tour enables you to decide for yourself.

Fall starts early in the Kingdom and spring arrives late, so if you're looking for autumn colors in mid-September, or unmowed green meadows in June, this is the tour to do.

DIRECTIONS FOR THE RIDE

0.0 From the Lyndonville post office at the intersection of US 5 (Broad Street) and Center Street, follow Center Street toward Lyndon Center and Lyndon State College.

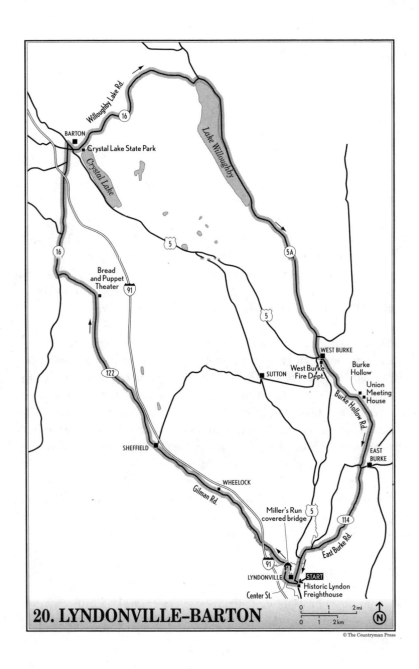

Willoughby Lake Rd.

16

BARTON

Crystal Lake State Park

Lake Willoughby

Crystal Lake

16

5

5A

Bread
and Puppet
Theater

91

5

122

WEST BURKE

West Burke
Fire Dept.

Burke
Hollow

SUTTON

Union
Meeting
House

Burke Hollow Rd.

EAST
BURKE

SHEFFIELD

WHEELOCK

Gilman Rd.

Miller's Run
covered bridge

5

114

East Burke Rd.

91

LYNDONVILLE

Center St.

START

Historic Lyndon
Freighthouse

0   1   2 mi
0   1   2 km

N

20. LYNDONVILLE–BARTON

Before you go or after you return, stop at the Historic Lyndon Freighthouse (1868), diagonally across Broad Street from the post office. The Freighthouse is among other things a restaurant, which serves breakfast all day, locally made baked goods, sand-wiches, Starbucks coffee, and Carmen's Ice Cream. You can build your own sundae and eat it at the antique soda fountain. The Freighthouse also displays hundreds of pictures that illustrate Lyndon's history, a model train display, and a rack of information about places of local interest.

Also look at the fabulous assortment of used books at Green Mountain Books, 1055 Broad Street.

On Wednesday evenings in the summer, the Lyndonville band performs on the village green. The Caledonia County Fair, which in true Vermont style combines livestock and horticultural exhibits with the attractions of a traveling carnival, happens in Lyndonville during August. For further information write the Lyndonville Town Clerk at 20 Park Avenue, Lyndonville, VT 05851, or call 802-626-5785.

0.5 At the T, turn right to continue on Center Street, which is unsigned here.

Within 0.5 mile, you pass Lyndon Institute on the left and go through Miller's Run cov-ered bridge (1878). Lyndon Institute was founded in 1867. It is a private, coeducational secondary school of approximately 630 students, of whom 35 are boarders. Like many other private schools in Vermont, Lyndon Institute also serves as a public school, educat-ing some pupils from Vermont towns that have no schools of their own. These towns pay the tuition for their students to attend the schools of their choice.

1.0 Turn left onto VT 122 North (Gilman Road).

In 5 miles you reach the tiny town of Wheelock. Its little green is shaded by 80-foot white pines and has a picnic table and hexagonal bandstand. In 1785, during Vermont's tenure as an independent nation (1777–1791), the General Assembly took the unusual action of granting land to a college in another country. Having no college of its own and wishing to ensure its sons an opportunity for learning, Vermont granted half the township of Wheelock to New Hampshire's Dartmouth College. As late as 1815 the rents that the cit-izens of Wheelock paid to Dartmouth accounted for a major portion of its revenue. Though Dartmouth no longer levies those rents, it does adhere to the policy it initiated in 1828 of charging no tuition to those sons and, more recently, daughters of Wheelock who are offered admission.

Three miles beyond Wheelock, VT 122 begins working its way uphill through Sheffield for 3.5 miles. The grade starts gently but turns steep in the final mile. The top of the hill marks the Connecticut River–Lake Champlain watershed; most rivers to the east flow into the former, while most of those to the west flow into the latter. Pause to look at the view behind you; on clear days you can see New Hampshire's Mount Washington. Then enjoy the rollicking 3-mile downhill run that lies ahead. Look out for moose!

The home of the Bread and Puppet Theater is 2 miles down the hill on your right. It's in a three-story red farmhouse across the road from a long, low shed. There may well be a hand-painted old school bus parked there as well. The hill is steep when you reach Bread and Puppet, so try not to go too fast.

Peter Schumann founded the Bread and Puppet Theater in 1962 on New York City's Lower East Side. Bread and Puppet moved to Vermont in 1970. This powerful, innovative company has, in its own words, presented "massive spectacles with 100 participants" in the United States, Europe, and Latin America. Its pageants, often performed outdoors, address "well-known social, political, and environmental issues or simply the common urgencies of our . . . age." By creating forceful dramatizations with extravagant papier-mâché figures, stilt walkers, and music, Bread and Puppet ridicules powerful governmental and commercial institutions and celebrates the poor, innocent, and humble. A Bread and Puppet performance is certain to be unique and full of fun.

Bread and Puppet has turned a hundred-year-old hay barn into a cavernous museum here. It houses scores of enormous masks, marvelous puppets, paintings, and other graphics. They make a striking scene in the dark barn. The museum is open May through October, 10–6 daily. Admission is free.

15.9 At the stop sign and T, turn right onto VT 16 North toward Barton.

20.4 At the traffic island in Barton, turn right onto US 5 South.

Before you leave, consider walking leftward across the street to the Pierce Block to visit the classic antique soda fountain at the Barton Pharmacy. You can get a real ice cream soda as well as coffee and sandwiches.

20.7 Turn left onto VT 16 East (Willoughby Lake Road).

If you're ready to swim or picnic, ride just 0.2 mile and turn right into the entrance to Crystal Lake State Park. There you'll find picnic tables and a swimming beach. Admission is charged.

A half mile beyond the park, VT 16 heads uphill for a mile. Three miles beyond the top, the road turns merrily downhill for 2.3 miles. Along the way, you have clear views of Mounts Hor and Pisgah, the mountain bookends on either side of Lake Willoughby. You'll soon be riding along its shoreline.

Lake Willoughby

27.8 At the stop sign, turn right onto VT 5A South toward West Burke.

You are now beside the swimming beach at the northern end of Lake Willoughby. A zillion years ago a monstrous glacier gouged this fjordlike lake out of the earth. It sits between the rocky faces of Mounts Hor (elevation 2,751 feet) and Pisgah (elevation 2,646 feet) and reaches depths of more than 300 feet. Its strikingly clear waters provide excellent swimming and fishing; they can be easily reached from the beaches at its northern and southern ends. The largest fish known to have been caught in Vermont on a rod and reel came from Lake Willoughby. It was a 35-pound, 44-inch lake trout caught on July 20, 2003.

In 2.8 miles you reach the start of the Mount Pisgah Trail on your left. It is 1.7 miles to the summit. By a quirk of nature, rare, delicate arctic plants grow on the cliffs of Mount Pisgah. Mostly calcicoles, which absorb the calcium they need from the rocks they cling to, these relics of the Ice Age find the moist, protected ledges of Pisgah hospitable.

39.2 In front of the West Burke Volunteer Fire Department, turn left onto Burke Hollow Road and follow it as it curves to the right.

The ride from West Burke through Burke Hollow is the most challenging of the tour. You climb a 0.7-mile hill in the first 2 miles and then a very steep hill of the same length just beyond Burke Hollow.

40.5 Follow Burke Hollow Road, which is unsigned here, as it curves to the left.

41.4 At the T, follow Burke Hollow Road, which is unsigned here, to the right.

In 150 yards you pass Union Meeting House on the left. The church and its delicate spire are unaltered, save fresh white paint, since their construction in 1825. It is worth stopping to look inside at the high barrel pulpit and old box pews, each with a separate door.

Just beyond the meetinghouse you encounter the very steep hill referred to above. The 0.7-mile climb can be difficult after riding more than 40 miles. From the top, you head nicely downhill for 2 miles.

44.2 At the stop sign, turn right onto VT 114 South (East Burke Road).

The village of East Burke is immediately to your left. You can eat at the River Garden Café or Pub Outback Restaurant; you can get a drink and snack at Bailey's and Burke General Store.

East Burke's Old School Museum stands 200 yards south of Bailey's on the same side of the road. This 18-by-23-foot retired schoolhouse contains a potpourri of items from its past: primers, pupils' desks, musical instruments, and a globe made by a local resident in about 1800. If the door is locked, you may be able to get a key at the Burke Mountain Clubhouse next door.

48.8 At the traffic light, turn left onto US 5 South.

49.5 At the blinking light, turn left to continue on US 5 South (Depot Street).

49.7 At the stop sign, turn right to continue on US 5 South (now Broad Street) and ride 50 yards to the Lyndonville post office (on your right), where you began.

Bicycle Repair Services

East Burke Sports, 439 VT 114, East Burke, VT (802-626-3215)

Great Outdoors Trading Company, 73 Main Street, Newport, VT (802-334-2831)

Peter Glenn of Vermont, 452 Railroad Street, St. Johnsbury, VT (802-748-3433)

Village Bike Shop, 3731 US 5, Derby, VT (802-766-8009)

Village Sport Shop, 511 Broad Street (US 5), Lyndonville, VT (802-626-8448)

IV. NORTHWESTERN VERMONT

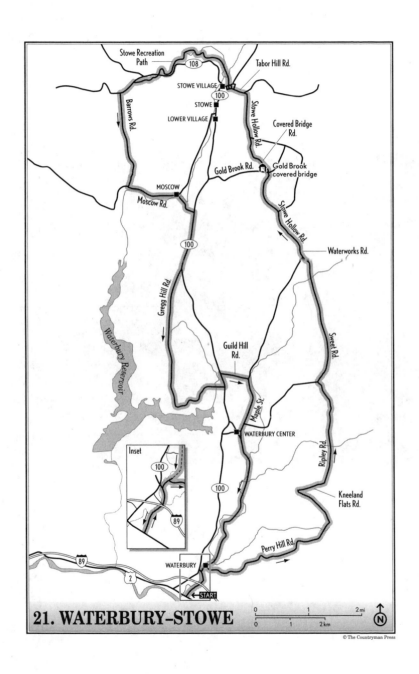

Stowe Recreation Path

108

Tabor Hill Rd.

STOWE VILLAGE

100

STOWE

LOWER VILLAGE

Barrows Rd.

Stowe Hollow Rd.

Covered Bridge Rd.

Gold Brook Rd.

Gold Brook covered bridge

MOSCOW

Moscow Rd.

100

Stowe Hollow Rd.

Waterworks Rd.

Waterbury Reservoir

Gregg Hill Rd.

Guild Hill Rd.

Sweet Rd.

Maple St.

WATERBURY CENTER

Ripley Rd.

Inset

100

89

100

Kneeland Flats Rd.

Perry Hill Rd.

89

2

WATERBURY

START

0   1   2 mi
0   1   2 km

21. WATERBURY–STOWE

N

© The Countryman Press

Waterbury–Stowe

MODERATE-TO-DIFFICULT TERRAIN; 31.2 MILES (15.1 MILES UNPAVED)

BEST RIDDEN ON A FAT-TIRED BICYCLE

This ride is worth the price of the book. It roams along the back roads of one of America's most famous resorts but stays far from the traffic. The views from these quiet back roads and two stretches of bicycle path rival the best in Vermont. And the hundreds of white birches clumped along the edges of the road bring to mind lines from Robert Frost's poem "Birches."

> When I see birches bend to left and right
> Across the lines of straighter darker trees,
> I like to think some boy's been swinging on them. . . .
> Some boy too far from town to learn baseball,
> Whose only play was what he found himself,
> Summer or winter, and could play alone. . . .
> I'd like to get away from earth awhile
> And then come back to it and begin over. . . .
> One could do worse than be a swinger of birches.

So let this lovely ride be your getaway from earth; you'll be back much too soon.

Nearly half the tour follows unpaved roads, which are most fun on a fat-tired bicycle. The unpaved roads are generally smooth and hard, and largely free of rocks. However, depending on recent weather, you may encounter some rough surfaces and occasional loose gravel. Bring a camera and a bathing suit and pack food for a picnic or grab something in Stowe, which is the halfway point. Once you get there, you have completed the challenging parts of the ride, for the second half of the tour goes mostly downhill.

Waterbury is the home of two of Vermont's best known brands, Green Mountain Coffee and Ben & Jerry's Homemade (founded in 1975 and purchased in 2000 by Unilever to much statewide consternation). If you'd like a close look at how Vermont's most famous ice cream is made, call 1-866-258-6877 for information about a factory tour. Ben & Jerry's is Vermont's most popular tourist attraction.

DIRECTIONS FOR THE RIDE

0.0 At the traffic light at the intersection of US 2 (Main Street) and Stowe Street, follow Stowe Street north.

0.7 Turn right onto Lincoln Street. If you miss this turn, you'll reach a traffic light on VT 100 in 30 yards.

0.8 Bear right onto Perry Hill Road.

In 0.2 mile you begin a substantial, 1.3-mile climb. Enjoy the increasingly panoramic views over your left shoulder as you work your way up and soon down. On a clear day you can see the peaks of Bolton Mountain (3,960 feet) and Mount Mansfield (4,393 feet), Vermont's highest, as well as several in between. The Long Trail, a hiking path that runs the length of the state, follows the ridge between these peaks.

When you reach the top of the hill, the road becomes unpaved. In 0.3 mile it heads downhill for a mile.

3.6 At the yield sign, turn left to continue on Perry Hill Road, which is unsigned here. Do not turn right onto Henry Hough Road.

In 0.2 mile, Perry Hill Road turns downhill for 0.7 mile, and you may encounter some small loose rocks. You will be looking straight at the ski slopes on Mount Mansfield, the foundation of Stowe's prosperity and celebrity.

4.5 At the stop sign, turn right onto Kneeland Flats Road, which is paved and immediately goes uphill.

4.6 Continue straight on Kneeland Flats Road; do not turn left onto Shaw Mansion Road. In 0.4 mile Kneeland Flats Road becomes unpaved.

As you make this, the tour's second, major climb—2.3 miles—you begin to see the distinctive cone-shaped top of Camels Hump (4,083 feet) on your left. The first 1.5 miles go nearly continuously up, and then the road makes several short, fairly steep rolls. One especially steep roll is paved. Along the way, Kneeland Flats Road changes name to Ripley Road.

Over the next 6 miles you ride past a variety of birch, beech, poplar, maple, fir, spruce, pine, and oak trees. Some interesting homes have been recently built on the nearby hillsides.

7.0 At the stop sign, turn right onto Sweet Road, which is unpaved. Do not be alarmed by the DEAD END sign, which is visible just as you make your turn. Unless to you are riding in the very early spring and the roads are muddy, you will have no difficulty getting through.

To the west you can see—from south to north—the peaks of Bone Mountain (2,896 feet), Woodward Mountain (3,100 feet), Ricker Mountain (3,398 feet), and Bolton Mountain (3,690 feet).

In 1.7 miles Sweet Road becomes a seasonal (or Class Four) road and changes name to Water Works Road. It narrows to a single lane, and the branches of the trees reach fully across it. Ride carefully and continue straight; do not turn onto any side roads. See if you can find the beaver pond on the left.

9.4 At the intersection, bear right uphill onto Stowe Hollow Road, which is unpaved and unsigned here.

You climb 0.3 mile. In another 0.2 mile, the road becomes paved for just 0.3 mile, which goes steeply downhill. Thereafter, the road is unpaved and the decent is more gradual. It lasts nearly a mile and a half. Near the end, the grade becomes steep again, heads around a sharp curve, and then suddenly ends. Be extremely cautious.

11.3 At the four-way intersection, stop and walk across Gold Brook Road onto Covered Bridge Road, which is unpaved.

Gold Brook Road heads uphill for a quarter mile and then down for a half mile. The Gold Brook covered bridge is 49 feet long. It was built in 1844 in the Howe Truss manner. If the water level is high, you can cool off in one of the large pools below the bridge.

12.1 At the stop sign, go straight onto Stowe Hollow Road, which is paved and unsigned here.

Stowe Hollow Road immediately heads downhill. In a quarter mile the descent becomes steep. You have a good view of Mount Mansfield through the trees on your left.

12.9 Turn left onto Tabor Hill Road, which heads downhill into Stowe.

13.2 At the intersection where the 1860 House Bed and Breakfast stands on you're right, turn left onto Pond Street. You immediately pass the Helen Day Memorial Library and Art Center on your left.

13.3 At the stop sign, turn right onto Park Street.

13.4 At the next stop sign, walk across Main Street (VT 100) onto the sidewalk. Turn right and walk 20 yards along the sidewalk to the far side of the Stowe Community Church (1863). There you can see a REC PATH PARKING sign. At the far end of the parking area, resume bicycling by getting onto the Stowe Recreation Path, which is paved.

You can obtain information about activities, special events, dining, lodging, and entertainment in Stowe from the visitor information center at 51 Main Street. Before leaving Stowe village, you may want to pick up food for a picnic or eat at one of the many restaurants. There are no more good opportunities for food until the tour is nearly over.

Along the rec path are many places to picnic and to swim, including an indoor Olympic-size swimming pool, called the Swimming Hole. The path is 5.5 miles long, crosses the West Branch several times, and avoids congested VT 108.

16.5 Get off the Stowe Recreation Path and turn right onto Luce Hill Road.

17.1 Turn left onto Barrows Road toward VT 100 and I-89

18.9 At the stop sign, turn left toward I-89 onto Moscow Road, which is unsigned here.

In a mile you reach the little burgh of Moscow that sports a general store and a couple of art galleries.

19.8 Bear right downhill and follow the signs toward VT 100 and I-89 so you continue on Moscow Road, which is unsigned here.

20.3 At the stop sign, turn right onto VT 100 South.

VT 100A may have a lot of traffic. Fortunately, the highway has a 3-foot, paved shoulder where you can ride.

21.3 Bear right onto Gregg Hill Road, which is unpaved.

Stowe Community Church (1863)

Gregg Hill Road goes largely downhill, occasionally steeply. At three places the descent takes a little turn upward, so you must climb a bit. Keep your speed under control and enjoy the lovely wooded landscape, ponds, and mountain views.

25.1 At the stop sign, turn left onto VT 100 North, which you take only 0.3 mile. Ride on the shoulder of the road.

25.4 Turn right onto Guild Hill Road.

You immediately ride up a very short hill and then head down.

25.9 At the stop sign, turn right onto Maple Street.

Maple Street goes largely downhill.

27.0 Do not turn right onto Howard Avenue. Instead continue straight for another 30 yards to the stop sign and there turn left onto Guptil Road.

Guptil Road is also largely downhill.

28.9 Just beyond Tanglewoods Restaurant (on your right), turn left onto Country Club Road, which is unpaved. If you miss this turn, you reach a stop sign at VT 100 in 0.1 mile.

29.2 At the top of the hill, bear right onto the Waterbury Community Path (often identified as WCP on maps), which is unpaved.

29.7 The Waterbury Community Path merges with Laurel Lane, which is unpaved.

30.0 Where Laurel Lane turns right, go straight back onto the Waterbury Community Path so you pass the private garage on your left.

30.2 Go straight onto Lincoln Street, which is unpaved for the first 100 yards. Do not turn onto Perry Hill Road.

30.5 At the stop sign, turn left onto Stowe Street.

31.2 At the traffic light, you are back in Waterbury at the intersection of US 2 (Main Street) and Stowe Street.

Bicycle Repair Services

AJ's Ski and Sport Shop, Mountain Road, Stowe, VT (802-253-4593)

Foot of the Notch Bicycles, 134 Church Street, Jeffersonville, VT (802-644-8182)

Irie Cycles, 409 Mountain Road, Stowe, VT (802-253-1947)

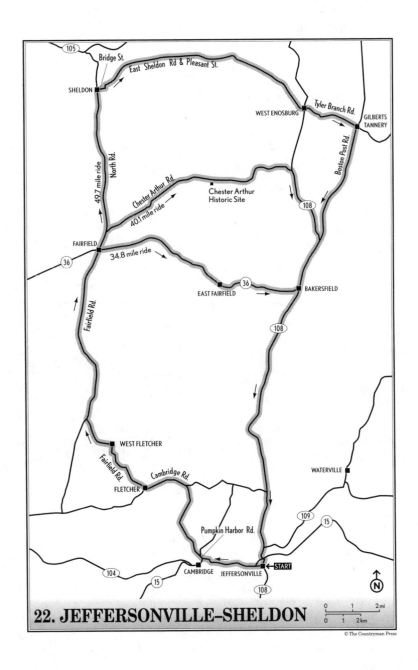

105
Bridge St.
East Sheldon Rd & Pleasant St.
SHELDON
Tyler Branch Rd.
WEST ENOSBURG
GILBERTS TANNERY
49.7 mile ride
North Rd.
Boston Post Rd.
Chester Arthur Rd.
Chester Arthur Historic Site
40.1 mile ride
108
FAIRFIELD
36
34.8 mile ride
EAST FAIRFIELD
36
BAKERSFIELD
108
Fairfield Rd.
WEST FLETCHER
WATERVILLE
Fairfield Rd.
Cambridge Rd.
FLETCHER
109
15
Pumpkin Harbor Rd.
104
CAMBRIDGE
JEFFERSONVILLE
START
15
108
N

0   1   2 mi
0   1   2 km

22. JEFFERSONVILLE–SHELDON

© The Countryman Press

Jeffersonville–Sheldon

MODERATE TERRAIN: 49.7 MILES (1.8 MILES UNPAVED)

MODERATE TERRAIN: 40.1 MILES (3.8 MILES UNPAVED)

MODERATE TERRAIN: 34.8 MILES

This tour suits an especially broad variety of bicyclists. The longest ride is a superb half-century. The 40.1-mile ride takes you over 3.8 miles of rough unpaved road—most pleasant on a fat-tired bicycle—to the reconstructed birthplace of President Chester A. Arthur. The 34.8-mile is considerably easier than the other two but just as remote.

Carved out of north-central Vermont, this tour uses back roads that avoid nearly all traffic. The landscape rightly feels remote, and it more closely resembles the Vermont of three decades ago than that of today. You ride by many farms—some large and prosperous, others small and hard-pressed. Splendid views of the Mount Mansfield range of the Green Mountains and the foothills of the Adirondacks seem to follow you. Whatever the ride may lack in architecture is more than compensated by the peacefulness and solitude of the rolling countryside.

The ride starts and finishes in Jeffersonville on the Lamoille River, at the foot of Mount Mansfield. The entire village is designated a National Historic District. Several of its oldest homes have been reborn as bed & breakfasts, art galleries, craft shops, or antiques stores. But unlike its nearby neighbor Stowe, "Jeff" retains a local, noncommercial flavor. The Mary Bryan Memorial Art Gallery, for example, is a mini-museum that displays changing exhibits of the work of local artists, and seems not the least bothered by the fact that it sits across the street from a noisy sawmill, ripping logs into two-by-fours.

Either before you start or after you finish, consider treating yourself to some of the excellent food at the Restaurant and Bakery at 158 Main Street.

DIRECTIONS FOR THE RIDE

0.0 At the intersection of VT 108 (Main Street) and Church Street in Jeffersonville, turn right onto Church Street. You immediately pass the Second Congregational United Church of Christ on your right.

In 1827, the local electorate voted to name its town Jeffersonville in honor of the nation's third president. Whether the citizens had short memories or just a quick change of heart, it is ironic that they chose to honor Thomas Jefferson. Twenty years earlier he had proposed the embargo of 1807–1809, which prohibited virtually all international trade and had infuriated most Vermonters, driving many to become smugglers. Indeed, just 8 miles south of Jeffersonville, the pass through the mountains is named Smugglers Notch.

0.3 At the stop sign and T, turn left onto VT 15 West. Ride cautiously on VT 15, for it may have considerable traffic.

2.2 At the blinking light, bear right onto Pumpkin Harbor Road, which becomes Cambridge Road. In a tenth of a mile you pass Bartlett Hill Road on your right.

Over the next 4.5 miles, you roll over four short hills and gain a net of 175 feet in elevation.

6.8 At the stop sign, go straight onto Fairfield Road.

In 0.2 mile you begin a climb that lasts 0.7 mile. A third of a mile farther on, the road turns downhill for 1.2 miles and soon becomes steep and winding; do not give into the temptation to go your fastest. Thereafter, the road climbs for about a mile and then goes downhill, often steeply, most of the way to the next turn. Along the way, do not turn onto either Howrigan Road (on your right) or Buck Hill Road (on your left).

16.5 At the blinking red light and stop sign (at Fairfield), go straight across VT 36 onto North Road, which may not be signed here. In just under four miles, do not turn left onto Pond Road.

Just 75 yards north of this intersection, you can get a sandwich or freshly baked goodie at Chester's bakery on the right.

More than a century ago, Fairfield was a bustling town of 1,700 citizens. The nearby port at St. Albans Bay on Lake Champlain had opened profitable southern markets to the local loggers and farmers. (Out-of-state markets are still the foundation of most successful Vermont businesses.) With the growth of commerce, little Fairfield sustained four physicians, three dry-goods stores, four gristmills, and three distilleries.

But Fairfield's most renowned export was Chester A. Arthur, the 21st president of the United States. Like the other Vermont-born president, Calvin Coolidge, Arthur made his career elsewhere (New York)—Coolidge made his in Massachusetts—and acceded to the presidency from the vice-presidency upon the death of the president.

Arthur was born in 1829, the fifth child of a fervent abolitionist preacher who moved from parish to parish in Vermont and New York. Arthur graduated from Union College in Schenectady, New York, in 1848; he then taught school, read the law, and joined a prominent New York City law firm.

Dignified, tall, and handsome, with a clean-shaven chin and prominent side-whiskers, Arthur looked like the late-19th-century president he became.

As a young man in New York, he worked diligently for the "Stalwart" Republican Party machine, controlled by Senator Roscoe Conkling. Recognizing the administrative genius that Arthur had demonstrated as quartermaster general of New York during the Civil War and his success as a lawyer, Conkling helped Arthur be appointed collector of customs at the Port of New York by President Ulysses S. Grant. The collector oversaw the movement of goods in New York harbor, collected duties and fines, and regulated the businesses of many merchants. A critical part of the job was to place supporters of the "Stalwart" machine into jobs at the port and then to collect money from them to support the machine. Arthur shined at all of this during a time when the political spoils system was under attack. Though apparently personally honest, Arthur believed in political patronage and routinely collected kickbacks from customs house employees to support the Republican Party.

In 1880, James Garfield and Arthur were elected president and vice president with just 48.4 percent of the popular vote, but a hefty majority of the electoral college. Then, almost immediately after taking office, Arthur broke with Garfield, when the latter appointed a reformer as collector of the Port of New York.

A year later, after succeeding to the presidency upon Garfield's assassination, Arthur surprised everyone by defying his reputation as a machine politician. Suddenly he began to support civil service reform and turned his back on political patronage and cronyism. He persuaded Congress to pass the Pendleton Act, which established a bipartisan Civil Service Commission, banned salary kickbacks, created a "classified system" to allocate some governmental positions through competitive written examinations, and protected federal employees from removal for partisan reasons.

Arthur next demonstrated independence from his party by vetoing the notorious transportation pork-barrel bill of 1882. He argued that the bill unduly benefited the South and that the federal surplus should be returned to the citizenry through tax reduction. He was enraged when Congress passed the bill over his veto.

Arthur also vetoed a proposed Chinese Exclusion Act, which would have banned Chinese immigration for 20 years. Arthur believed that Chinese immigrants had made great economic contributions to America, especially by their work building the transcontinental railroad. He also thought the bill would jeopardize America's access to the potentially rich Chinese market. When Congress decreased the ban to 10 years, Arthur signed the bill.

The fourth major area where Arthur marched to a different drummer was trade protection. Late-19th-century Republicans—in contrast to the Democrats—generally supported high tariff rates to protect big business and manufacturing. Instead Arthur pushed tariff reduction to relieve indebted farmers and middle-class consumers.

Although domestic affairs dominated the Arthur presidency, he initiated the construction of a modern navy of steam-powered, steel ships.

Yet Arthur was no simple Vermont idealist. As collector of the Port of New York in the 1870s, he had become a very wealthy man. He acquired elegant tastes and loved to throw lavish parties. By the time he became president, Arthur was known as "The Gentleman Boss." Disgusted by the shabby look of the White House, Arthur hired New York's most famous designer, Louis Tiffany, to transform it into a showplace.

In 1884 the Republican Party refused to nominate Arthur for president, and he died two years later.

Publisher Alexander K. McClure recalled, "No man ever entered the Presidency so profoundly and widely distrusted, and no one ever retired . . . more generally respected."

34.8-MILE RIDE: Instead of going straight onto North Road, turn right onto VT 36 East and ride 7.9 miles to the stop sign. The terrain has several rolls, but none are steep or very long. At the stop sign (at Bakersfield), turn right onto VT 108 South and ride 9.6 miles. Then resume following the directions below from mileage 48.9.

40.1-MILE RIDE: Go straight onto North Road, but ride only 0.7 mile. Then, as you descend a small hill, turn right toward the Chester Arthur Historic Site onto Chester Arthur Road, which may be unsigned here, and ride 8.5 miles to the stop sign. In a mile the road tips downhill for 0.7 mile and then goes up for 1.2 miles. It becomes unpaved 4.8 miles from where the road began; the road surface is rough, and though it can be ridden on any sort of bicycle, it is easiest on a fat-tired one.

A half mile farther on, the Chester Arthur Birthplace is on your right. It is open late-May through mid-October, 11–5 Wednesday through Sunday. This tiny two-room parsonage was reconstructed in 1953 from photographs; it is unfurnished but contains a display of words and photographs. Its 480 square feet accommodated seven persons in 1830, but of course it had no indoor plumbing! It is also the only presidential birthplace still on an unpaved road.

Birthplace of President Chester Arthur

From the Arthur house continue east on Chester Arthur Road. The road initially goes downhill for 0.5 mile, then up for a mile, and finally down two hills, the first 0.9 mile and the second 0.8 mile. Ride cautiously on the descents; the final two get steep.

At the stop sign, turn right onto VT 108 South, which is paved but unsigned here. Follow VT 108 South for 13.6 miles, and then resume following the directions from mileage 48.9 below.

22.2 At the stop sign (in Sheldon), turn right onto Bridge Street, which becomes East Sheldon Road.

In October 1864, after an attack on St. Albans, 22 Confederate soldiers came through Sheldon on their retreat to Canada. They set a Sheldon covered bridge ablaze, but alert village citizens saved it. In their haste to escape from the aroused villagers, the Confederates abandoned their plan to rob the local bank.

22.5 Do not turn left onto Church Street. Continue just past it and bear left to continue on East Sheldon Road; do not go straight onto Bridge Road. In 0.3 mile, East Sheldon Road becomes Pleasant Street, which goes uphill for 0.3 mile, and then changes name back to East Sheldon Road.

East Sheldon Road follows a ridge, which offers grand views to the north, and goes down, then up, and then down, each time for 0.7 mile.

29.1 At the stop sign, go straight across Duffy Hill Road to continue on East Sheldon Road, which is now not paved.

The surface is hard but may have some loose gravel on it.

30.9 Go straight across West Enosburg Road (VT 108) onto Tyler Branch Road, which is paved.

33.0 At the stop sign at the crossroad, turn right onto Boston Post Road.

The next four miles roll up and down.

37.3 At the stop sign, turn left onto VT 108 South.

VT 108 goes immediately uphill for 0.5 mile, levels off as you pass through the tiny village of Bakersfield, and then heads mostly downhill for much of 9 miles.

48.9 Go straight to continue on VT 108 South toward VT 15 and Jeffersonville.

49.3 At the blinking light, go straight across VT 15 to continue on VT 108 South (Main Street), which will take you into Jeffersonville.

49.7 You are back at the intersection of VT 108 (Main Street) and Church Street, where you began.

Bicycle Repair Services

AJ's Ski Shop, Mountain Road, Stowe, VT (802-253-4593)

Foot of the Notch Bicycles, 134 Church Street, Jeffersonville, VT (802-644-8182)

Mountain Sports and Bike Shop, Mountain Road, Stowe, VT (802-253-7971)

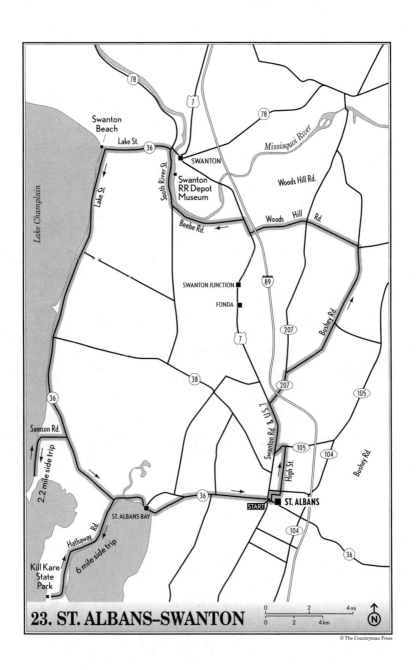

23. ST. ALBANS–SWANTON

© The Countryman Press

St. Albans–Swanton

EASY TERRAIN; 28.7 MILES PLUS SIDE TRIPS OF 2.2 AND 6 MILES

St. Albans is a small, quiet, 19th-century city with great redbrick architecture. The city faces Taylor Park, perhaps Vermont's most grand town green. It is shaded by enormous trees and sports a long reflecting pool, a circular fountain, and a handsome bandstand. Give yourself time to enjoy it.

The tour follows quiet roads without hills or much traffic through expansive farmlands, along the Missisquoi River and the northern shore of Lake Champlain. Henry Ward Beecher thought St. Albans sat "in the midst of a greater variety of scenic beauty than any other [place] I can remember in America." Although this corner of Vermont has witnessed many changes in the one hundred years since Beecher was writing, it remains very beautiful, tranquil, and charming.

This tour ideally suits families with children. After a very little bit of climbing on the way out of St. Albans, the riding is easy and panoramic. There's lots to see and do: hundreds of waterfowl, especially in the fall; a restored 19th-century railroad station; and several places to swim and picnic. The tour also lends itself to cycling in the early and late parts of the season, for Lake Champlain tempers the climate, hastening spring and stalling the fall. With no leaves on the trees the views are even more spectacular, and with fewer vacationers about, the roads are nearly yours alone. If you ride in April, you can also visit the Vermont Maple Sugar Festival in St. Albans. It's a joyous occasion, with sugar on snow, lumberjack contests, square dances, pancake breakfasts, a fiddling contest, and much more. If you ride on a Saturday between May and October, you can visit the St. Albans Farmers Market.

For breakfast try Kartula's Café and Bagel Bakery or the Park Café, both on the west side of Main Street. Consider carrying food along for lunch; there are several ideal places to picnic and little to purchase along the way.

DIRECTIONS FOR THE RIDE

0.0 From the traffic light on Main Street (US 7) at the southwestern corner of Taylor Park, ride uphill on Fairfield Street (VT 36 East).

By leaving St. Albans on residential roads, rather than US 7, the tour avoids traffic and takes you past some wonderful public buildings and handsome homes.

Because of its proximity to Canada, St. Albans has witnessed some curious events. Before the railroad reached here, potash was the city's only salable product, and Montreal its only market. But in 1807 the passage of Thomas Jefferson's Embargo Act outlawed trade with all foreign nations, and the good folk of St. Albans became deeply involved in smuggling. One local merchant hired a craft, named Black Snake, *to run potash into Canada. His business thrived for several months until the border patrol discovered* Black Snake *and chased it down Lake Champlain. At Burlington a bloody battle ensued, and the smugglers killed three federal officers and wounded several others before losing their craft. Opposition to the Embargo Act ran so deep in Vermont that only one smuggler was executed. The others were imprisoned and subsequently pardoned.*

With the completion of the railroad in 1850, prosperity came to St. Albans. But prosperity also set the stage for the most memorable day in St. Albans's history. At three o'clock in the afternoon of October 19, 1864, 22 rebel soldiers seeking funds for the Confederacy converged on St. Albans. They entered all the banks simultaneously, unburdened them of more than $200,000, killed one man, and wounded several others. The rebels then burned the Sheldon covered bridge and hustled their booty across the border to Canada. Thus did St. Albans become the site of the northernmost engagement of the Civil War.

Mementos of the raid, including photographs, some of the stolen currency, and a broadside entitled "Orleans County Awake, Rebels in Vermont!" are exhibited at the St. Albans Historical Museum, which faces the eastern edge of Taylor Park. The museum's large and diverse collection also contains two interesting medical exhibits. One consists of the memorabilia of William Beaumont, a surgeon who studied in St. Albans from 1810 to 1812. Beaumont made a significant contribution to medical research by reporting on the digestive system of a patient who had a permanent hole in his stomach from a gunshot wound. The other exhibit contains furnishings from Dr. George Russell's Arlington, Vermont, office. Norman Rockwell made this country doctor's office famous in his painting The Family Doctor. It was first published as a cover of The Saturday Evening Post in 1947. The museum also contains period costumes and railroad memorabilia. It is open Tuesday through Saturday 1–4 during July and August and by appointment; call 802-527-7933. Admission is charged.

0.1 Turn left onto Church Street and ride north along Taylor Park.

On your right in the following order are: St. Luke's Episcopal Church, the St. Albans Historical Museum, St. Paul's United Methodist Church, the Franklin County Courthouse, and the Romanesque First Congregational Church.

First Congregational Church, St. Albans

0.2 At the stop sign, turn right onto Bank Street, which goes uphill.

0.3 At the stop sign, turn left onto High Street.

You will encounter five stop signs over the next mile. At each one, go straight to continue on High Street.

1.4 At the stop sign at the T, turn left onto VT 105 South, which is unsigned here. Ride downhill just 100 yards and then go straight off VT 105 onto Seymour Road.

1.6 At the stop sign, turn right onto Swanton Road (US 7 North).

Bicycling on US 7 requires your complete attention. There is no shoulder, and traffic may be heavy.

2.2 At the traffic light, continue straight on Swanton Road.

2.4 At the next traffic light, continue straight on Swanton Road.

2.6 Turn right onto VT 207 North toward Highgate Center.

In a quarter mile, you go uphill for a half mile as you ride beneath I-89.

3.4 Turn right onto Bushey Road.

6.9 At the stop sign, turn left onto Woods Hill Road.

Woods Hill Road goes gently downhill for 1.3 miles.

8.0 At the stop sign, go straight across Highgate Road (VT 207) to continue on Woods Hill Road.

In 0.7 mile, Woods Hill Road starts down a hill that gets steep as it passes beneath I-89. Keep your speed down, for there's a stop sign at the bottom of the hill.

9.4 At the stop sign, turn right onto US 7 North.

9.7 Just beyond the cemetery on your left, turn left onto Beebe Road.

Over the next two miles you follow the Missisquoi River toward Lake Champlain. Missisquoi means "much grass" and "many waterfowl." The Missisquoi National Wildlife Refuge, fewer than 5 miles away, covers 4,792 acres of marshland, so you may see some interesting wildlife. More than 180 species of birds—including osprey, great horned owl, bald eagle, and great blue heron—have been sighted in the refuge.

11.4 At the stop sign, bear right onto South River Street. Be sure to keep the Missisquoi River on your right; do not cross the railroad tracks.

In a mile you reach the Swanton Historical Society and Railroad Depot Museum on the left. Make sure you stop. It's usually open between 11 and 3 Tuesday through Saturday. This restored 1875 railroad station is a delight, and it displays a charming collection of railroad memorabilia. Ladies and gentlemen used separate waiting rooms in the station to shield the fairer sex from the men's foul speech and spitting. Outside under tall shade trees you can picnic at a table in the center of the stone foundation of the old roundhouse!

12.7 Turn left onto Lake Street (VT 36). In 0.1 mile you cross a set of railroad tracks. You can easily miss this turn; if you do, you reach a stop sign in 75 yards.

Like St. Albans, Swanton is no stranger to smuggling. Bootleggers of the Roaring 20s who hauled Canadian whiskey into Swanton were the spiritual descendants of the Vermont farmers who drove cattle into Canada to sell to the starving British soldiers during the War of 1812.

Each year near the end of July, Swanton produces a festival that includes arts and crafts exhibits, band concerts, barbershop-quartet singing, a lumberjack roundup, a chicken barbecue, a parade, and a fairway with rides and concessions. For details and a schedule, write the Swanton Chamber of Commerce at Box 182, Swanton, VT 05488, or call 802-868-7200.

A mile and a half after turning onto Lake Street, just as Lake Champlain comes into view, you reach Swanton Beach on your right. It's a good place for lunch. You may picnic on the broad lawn that borders the lake. There is also easy access to the water for a swim, though the first 20 yards from shore are weedy.

Lake Champlain is the sixth largest body of fresh water in the United States. It covers 435 square miles and stretches 118 miles along Vermont's western border with New York as well as 17 miles into Québec, Canada. In the winter the lake usually freezes to a depth of 2 feet and supports a multitude of fishing shanties. Although private homes, cottages, and trees occasionally obstruct your view along this stretch of road, you can often see across the lake to the Adirondack Mountains. A mile and a quarter after the road pulls away from the lakeshore, Camels Hump (elevation 4,083 feet), Vermont's fourth highest peak, comes into view far in the southeast. Once you know its name, you can always identify it.

20.8 2.2-MILE SIDE TRIP: *At the crossroad—6.5 miles south of Swanton Beach— turn right onto Samson Road. Samson Road heads west through a meadow to the* lakeshore and then follows the shoreline for a shaded 0.7 mile. It's a lovely ride. No buildings stand between the road and the lake, and the views westward are wonderful. This section of Lake Champlain is called the Inland Sea, since it is nearly entirely separated from the remainder of the lake by islands and sandbars. The water along this shore is especially clear. Retrace your way back to VT 36 and continue southward.

24.9   6-MILE SIDE TRIP: 1.8 miles farther south on VT 36, you reach Hathaway Road on the right. It goes to Kill Kare State Park, 3 miles away. The ride is easy and delightful; it follows the shoreline of St. Albans Bay for 2 miles. Kill Kare is a great destination, whether for a meal, swimming, or just relaxation. The park sits on a spit of land at the southern end of Hathaway Point. Rolling lawns are bounded by the lake on three sides. The park provides barbecuing grills, a beach, swings for young children, and toilet facilities. Try to arrive late in the afternoon and stay to cook a barbecue. From Kill Kare you can catch a boat to Burton Island State Park, which offers even better swimming as well as good fishing and camping.

25.3 Ride 180 degrees around the rotary to continue on VT 36 East.

25.8 Bear right off VT 36 onto Georgia Shore Road.

26.1 Turn left onto Church Road. Do not turn onto Little Country Road or Patten Crosby Road.

26.8 At the stop sign, turn right back onto VT 36 East (Lake Street), which is unsigned here. You immediately pass a cemetery on your right and ride uphill for a mile.

28.7 At the traffic light, you are back in front of Taylor Park in St. Albans, where the ride began.

Along Main Street you can find ice cream treats at Sweet Nothings, good books and magazines at Better Planet Books, and delicious meals at Jeff's Seafood, Bar & Grill and Chow! Bella.

Bicycle Repair Services

Foot of the Notch Bicycles, Church Street (VT 108), Jeffersonville, VT (802-644-8182)

Porter's Bike Shop, 116 Grand Avenue, Swanton, VT (802-868-7417)

24

Alburg–Isle La Motte

EASY TERRAIN; 34.7 MILES (1.4 MILES UNPAVED)

EASY TERRAIN; 22.8 MILES (1.4 MILES UNPAVED)

The northwestern corner of Vermont is its most panoramic and perhaps its most blissful, for here you are at the center of the Lake Champlain basin. Lush, flat farmland spreads across the landscape; the Green Mountains stand as a sentinel at the eastern horizon, as do the Adirondacks in the west. Lake Champlain itself runs up the center, and the towns are very small and quiet. Cycling along America's sixth largest lake, you can see for more than a hundred miles. The terrain is easy and the traffic light. These roads are especially well suited for beginning riders and families with children. But the strongest cyclists will find the tour's peacefulness and beauty just as wonderful.

The tour follows the bucolic shorelines of two islands: Isle La Motte and North Hero. You nearly always ride within sight of the water, and when you're not, you can usually see mountains instead. Because the route changes directions so often, it is fun to take along a compass, but it is not needed. Along with panoramic views and excellent swimming, the tour leads to some charming black marble and stone architecture, the oldest coral reef in the world, and the site of the first Catholic Mass in North America (1666). If you ride during July or August, you can also see the Royal Lipizzan stallions perform. Call 802-372-8400 for information.

DIRECTIONS FOR THE RIDE

0.0 From the Town of Alburg Municipal Offices, follow US 2 East. Sometimes

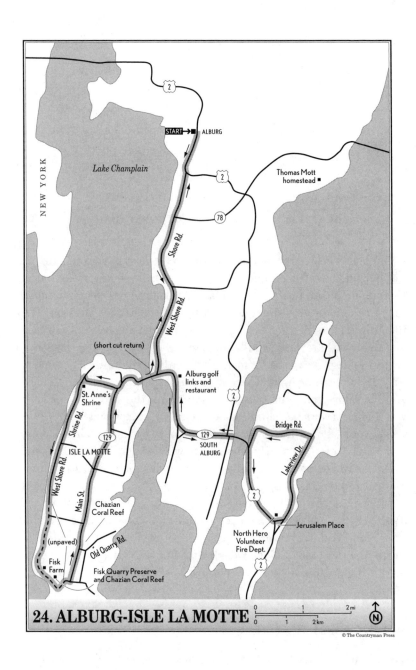

NEW YORK

Lake Champlain

2

START ■→ ALBURG

2

78

Thomas Mott
homestead ■

Shore Rd.

West Shore Rd.

(short cut return)

Alburg golf
links and
restaurant ■

2

St. Anne's
Shrine ■

Shrine Rd.

129

ISLE LA MOTTE

West Shore Rd.

Main St.

Chazian
Coral Reef

(unpaved)

Fisk
Farm ■

Old Quarry Rd.

Fisk Quarry Preserve
and Chazian Coral Reef

129

SOUTH
ALBURG

Bridge Rd.

Lakeview Dr.

2

Jerusalem Place

North Hero
Volunteer
Fire Dept. ■

2

24. ALBURG-ISLE LA MOTTE

| 0 | | 1 | | 2 mi |

| 0 | 1 | 2 km |

N

Alburg is spelled with a final "h."

Like many other Vermont towns along the U.S.-Canadian border, but especially those on Lake Champlain, Alburg has seen its share of smuggling. During the winter, it was easy to pull contraband over the ice that separated the two countries. One story tells of an Alburg smuggler whose load crashed into the freezing water when the ice below him broke. The quick Vermonter saved himself, but his clothes were so drenched that they immediately froze stiff. Unable to mount his horse or even walk, the savvy outlaw threw himself on the ice, clutched the trailing harness, and made his horses drag him to salvation.

Three miles from here, the healing waters at Alburg Springs were an important destination for mid-19th-century travelers from New York and southern New England. The health faddists of that day traveled by train to "take the waters" here, as they did at more than a dozen other mineral springs around Vermont.

You can get breakfast, sandwiches to go, or ice cream treats at the Alburg Country Store and Deli on your right as you head out of town.

0.7 Turn right toward St. Anne's Shrine and Isle La Motte onto Shore Road.

You are immediately riding along the western coast of New England. Lake Champlain flows northward—unlike most North American lakes—118 miles from Whitehall, New York, to Canada. With 435 square miles of surface and depths to 400 feet, Champlain was once the principal transportation route between New York City and Montreal. Now pleasure boats dominate the lake. They can travel up the Hudson, through 12 locks at Whitehall, New York, through the New York State Barge Canal into Lake Champlain, and then north onto the Richelieu River to Montreal.

Scores of species of fish live in the lake: Bass, walleye, yellow perch, northern pike, lake trout, and landlocked salmon are the most popular. And nearly everyone is still seeking positive identification of "Champ," the lake's elusive long-necked monster. In the winter, when the lake freezes deep enough to drive across, hardy Vermonters pull their fishing shanties onto the ice to catch the sweetest smelt and perch a frying pan ever saw.

5.2 At the stop sign, turn right onto VT 129 West toward St. Anne's Shrine and Isle La Motte.

Great historical dramas have played out upon this lakeshore. Samuel de Champlain wrote that he camped and hunted here on July 2 and 3, 1609. In 1665, swashbuckling French gallants, under the direction of a Captain de La Motte, built a fort here. Just a year later, adventuresome Jesuits celebrated the first Catholic Mass in the North American wilderness where St. Anne's Shrine now stands. More than a century later, in

1776, Benedict Arnold set sail off the western shore of the island for Valcour Island to battle the British. Only a year before, Arnold had accompanied Ethan Allen and the Green Mountain Boys in their successful attack on Fort Ticonderoga.

6.2 Turn right toward St. Anne's Shrine onto Shrine Road; you reach St. Anne's Shrine in a mile. From the shrine continue south on West Shore Road so that you keep Lake Champlain on your right. Do not turn onto School Street, which you reach in 2.2 miles. West Shore Road becomes unpaved in 2.4 miles and remains unpaved for 1.4 miles. The surface is hard.

St. Anne's Shrine stands on the site once occupied by Fort St. Anne, the first European (and French) settlement (1666) in what is now Vermont. Nestled among lofty pines at the edge of the lake, the shrine invites you to pause for reflection and rest. Eucharist celebrations are offered daily in a simple open-air structure. The Edmundite fathers and brothers who oversee the shrine also maintain a sandy public beach, picnic tables, and a snack bar. The shrine is open May 15 to October 15.

Also on this site is a grand granite statue of Samuel de Champlain and an unidentified

St. Anne's Shrine, Isle La Motte

Native American. It commemorates Champlain's 1609 landing on Isle La Motte.

Four miles beyond St. Anne's, you reach the beautiful Fisk Farm on your left. This small settlement of stone, black marble, and clapboard buildings is no longer a working farm. A remarkable woman, Linda Vaughn Fitch, has transformed it into a peaceful sanctuary where all are welcome to relax and enjoy the setting. "Fisk Farm is a metaphor," she writes, "A challenge to rise up and create something out of rotting timbers, old dreams, and moments of cathedral-like inspiration."

On Sunday afternoons, 1–5, Linda and her friends host a Tea Garden with art shows in the barn and musical performances—usually classical or folk, but sometimes jazz. "We love cyclists! No matter how casually dressed or hot. They can cool off with iced tea or lemonade!" (For more information log on to www.fiskfarm.com/events.)

Just beyond the farm, on your left, is the Fisk Quarry Preserve, which contains a section of the famous Chazian Coral Reef. It is the world's oldest known reef in which corals appear. A kiosk at the end of the pedestrian path there describes the geological history of this formation and its more recent past as Vermont's oldest quarry. It is owned by the Isle La Motte Preservation Trust.

12.5 At the intersection just after the road becomes paved, go straight onto Main Street. The street sign is partially hidden on the left.

At the next intersection—in 0.6 mile—you reach a small stone building on your right that houses the Isle La Motte Historical Society. Immediately north of this intersection is an overgrown pasture, where you can also see many pale gray outcroppings of the Chazian Reef. They are dramatic evidence that deep oceans once covered the Champlain valley. To get a good look at the reef and its fossils, you must walk into the pasture; and to do that you need permission from Tom LaBombard. He can be reached at 802-928-3707. If you do walk into the pasture, be sure not to disturb or damage any part of the reef or fossils, and beware of poison ivy.

15.0 At the crossroad in Isle La Motte village, continue straight onto VT 129 East (Main Street).

17.3 At the T, just beyond the causeway you crossed at mile 5.2, bear right to continue on VT 129. You have now completely circled Isle La Motte. The water is on your right, and you pass a small cemetery on your left in 0.1 mile.

In 0.4 mile you reach the entrance to Alburg Golf Links and Restaurant on your left. Lunch and dinner are served there. About a mile beyond Alburg Golf, you ride up a gentle grade for 0.5 mile.

North and South Hero are named after the heroic Vermonters who fought in the

Revolutionary War. In 1779, the independent nation of Vermont granted the two largest islands in Lake Champlain to Ethan Allen, Samuel Herrick, and 363 other Revolutionary War veterans.

FOR THE 22.8-MILE RIDE: Do not turn right at the T. Instead turn left onto Shore Road and retrace your way back to Alburg. Follow Shore Road 4.5 miles to the stop sign. There, turn left onto US 2 West and ride 0.7 mile to the Town of Alburg Municipal Offices (on your left).

20.1 At the stop sign (at the end of VT 129), turn right onto US 2 East.

22.2 Just 0.1 mile beyond the North Hero Volunteer Fire Department (on your left), turn left onto Jerusalem Place. Look carefully for this turn and walk across US 2.

22.3 At the stop sign, turn left onto Lakeview Drive. The lake is now on your right.

24.5 Turn left onto Bridge Road.

26.3 At the stop sign, turn right onto US 2 West.

26.7 Turn left onto VT 129 West toward Isle La Motte. You have now completed your visit to North Hero Island and are headed back toward Alburg.
In 2.4 miles you again pass the Alburg Golf Links and Restaurant, now on your right.

29.4 Turn right onto West Shore Road. The lake is now on your left. Do not turn left toward Isle la Motte.

33.9 At the stop sign, turn left onto US 2 West.

34.7 You are back at the Town of Alburg Municipal Offices (now on your left), where you began.

Bicycle Repair Services

Foot of the Notch Bicycles, Church Street (VT 108), Jeffersonville, VT (802-644-8182)

Porter's Bike Shop, 116 Grand Avenue, Swanton, VT (802-868-7417)

White's Green Mountain Bikes, 1008 Ethan Allen Highway (US 7), Georgia, VT (802-524-4496)

25

Montgomery–Richford

MODERATE-TO-DIFFICULT TERRAIN; 22.6 OR 33.7 MILES

The best is left for last. There is no ride I enjoy more than this one. Beginning just eight miles from Canada, this tour offers everything a hardy cyclist could want: extraordinary beauty, roads free of traffic, and a perfect balance of challenge and exhilaration. It is also the only tour to cross an international border.

The route winds through rolling farmlands fringed by thousands of sugar maples and bounded by the mountains. The longer ride curves into Canada for five miles and climbs a major hill in the midst of miles of well-tended apple orchards, an aromatic treat in May and a juicy treat in late September. Falling at the northern end of the Green Mountains, the route is relatively hilly, though it never crosses a mountain pass. But the undulating terrain provides outstanding downhill runs and countless sweeping views of the mountains. Both routes begin with an easy ride past two covered bridges on the Trout River and culminate in a crescendo of hard work and thrilling reward as you sweep through a third covered bridge.

DIRECTIONS FOR THE RIDE

0.0 From the Black Lantern Inn in Montgomery, follow VT 118 North.

Deb Winters, the innkeeper of the Black Lantern, is happy to have you park there. But she asks that you please go into the inn to tell her you are doing so.

Off the southwestern side of VT 118—to your left as you leave Montgomery—two covered bridges cross the Trout River. Sheldon and Savannah Jewett built them both. Each one is 80 feet long and shades good swimming and fishing. Both are on your left.

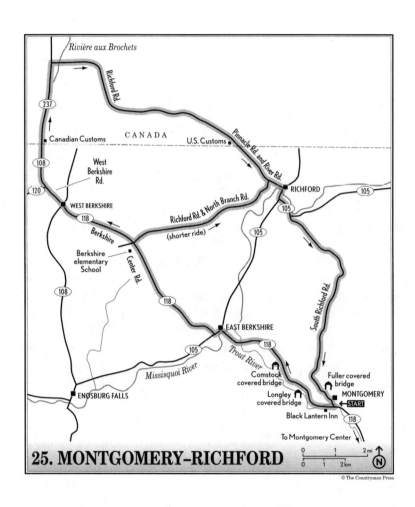

Rivière aux Brochets

Richford Rd.

237

CANADA

Canadian Customs

U.S. Customs

Pinnacle Rd. and River Rd.

108

West
Berkshire
Rd.

120

RICHFORD

105

WEST BERKSHIRE

118

Richford Rd. & North Branch Rd.

105

Berkshire

(shorter ride)

105

Berkshire
elementary
School

Center Rd.

108

118

South Richford Rd.

EAST BERKSHIRE

118

105

Trout River

Comstock
covered bridge

Fuller covered
bridge

Missisquoi River

Longley
covered bridge

MONTGOMERY
START

ENOSBURG FALLS

Black Lantern Inn

118

To Montgomery Center

25. MONTGOMERY–RICHFORD

0   1   2 mi
0   1   2 km

N

You reach the first, known as Longley or Harnois Bridge, one mile from Montgomery; it went into use in 1863. The second, the Comstock Bridge, was erected 20 years later and is visible 1.5 miles after the first.

4.8 At the stop sign and T in East Berkshire, turn left to continue on VT 118 North, ride just 75 yards, and turn right to continue on VT 118 North (Berkshire Center Road).

About 1.5 miles of the next 2.5 go uphill. Along the way, stop to look at the views behind you. To the east stands Jay Peak (3,861 feet), readily identifiable by its cone-shaped top on which a ski lift is perched.

You're now just 6 miles east of Enosburg Falls, one of only a few towns chartered by the Republic of Vermont during its 14 years as an independent nation (1777–1791). Enosburg Falls is now best known for maple syrup and the Vermont Dairy Festival. The festival takes place on the village green on the first Friday, Saturday, and Sunday of June. It features a parade, livestock shows, horse-pulling contests, barbecues, and lots of country fiddling and square dancing. Since the festival draws considerable traffic, and VT 105 has no shoulder, it's best not to ride there. But it is fun to combine an early springtime ride with a visit to the Dairy Festival.

In the early 19th century an Enosburg settler named Isaac Farrar developed wooden spouts to tap sugar-maple trees. Though the effectiveness of the spouts quickly led to their widespread use, Farrar's neighbors still accused him of "scientific farming," which then was not the vogue it has become. Later in the 19th century Enosburg Falls acquired a substantial reputation as the home of patent medicines, "guaranteed" to cure nearly every ill of man and beast. At least four local entrepreneurs amassed fortunes with their cures, and some people say that descendants of the original manufacturers still pursue the business.

9.0 At the crossroad by the Berkshire Elementary School (on your left), go straight to continue on VT 118 North (Berkshire Center Road). Much of the next 2 miles rolls downhill.

22.6-MILE RIDE: At the crossroad by the Berkshire Elementary School, do not go straight. Instead turn right onto Richford Road, which becomes North Branch Road.

For a mile you climb a moderate grade. Then the road turns downward into a glorious four-mile descent facing one of the most panoramic views in Vermont. Before you stands the Jay Peak range; to your left in Canada is the hump of Pinnacle Mountain; and on the clearest days Mount Mansfield, at 4,393 feet Vermont's tallest summit, is visible far to the south, over your right shoulder.

Ride 4.7 miles to the T and there turn right onto Pinnacle Road, which becomes River Road. You immediately cross a bridge. In 0.2 mile on the right there is a grassy picnic area overlooking the Missisquoi River. Follow River Road just 0.5 mile to the stop sign and blinking light in Richford. From there, resume following the directions below from mileage 25.5.

11.7 At the end of VT 118 in West Berkshire, go straight onto VT 108 North (West Berkshire Road) toward Frelighsburg, Québec.

12.3 At the intersection with VT 120, go straight to continue on VT 108 North.

Eleven miles northwest of here, at Eccles Hill in Québec, the Fenians—a secret Irish brotherhood organized in the 1850s to gain independence for Ireland—marshaled an attack on Canada in 1870. Nearly one thousand Fenians came to Vermont by train from Boston. They fought one small battle—the only violent encounter of their unsuccessful attempt to acquire land for a New Ireland—and then fled back into the United States, where a federal marshal promptly arrested their leaders.

13.8 Report to Canadian Customs at the international border. After you leave customs, the road becomes Québec 237 Nord.

For years, if not centuries, the United States and Canada have allowed their citizens to cross the Canadian border with only a driver's license as identification. Unfortunately, in 2004 Congress passed and President George W. Bush signed the Western Hemisphere Travel Initiative. This law requires that, beginning on January 1, 2008, all individuals must present passports or equivalent documents proving identity and citizenship when crossing a land border between the United States and Canada or Mexico.

16.2 Turn right onto Richford Road toward Abercorn. You immediately cross the Rivière aux Brochets.

In a half mile you can see Pinnacle Mountain on your left and the heart-pounding hill you will soon be climbing. Though it's only a mile long, it's a major climb. Apple orchards and a few cornfields stretch for miles along both sides of the road, making this area especially aromatic in May and colorful in September. Shortly after you reach the top and begin your two-mile descent into Richford, mountains of nearby Québec and Vermont fill the horizon.

Looking south toward Mount Mansfield from Richford

23.7 Report to U.S. Customs at the international border.

The road drops into a delicious descent, but keep your speed under control. You reach a stop sign in 1.3 miles while you are still descending.

25.0 At the stop sign, go straight onto Pinnacle Road, which becomes River Road.

You immediately cross a bridge. In 0.2 mile on the right there is a grassy picnic area overlooking the Missisquoi River.

25.5 At the stop sign and blinking light, turn right onto Main Street, which is unsigned here, and cross the bridge into Richford.

Richford stands in the midst of enormous natural beauty, but the village bears the scars of misfortune and adversity. More than once ravaged by fire or flood, Richford has also suffered recent economic hardship. Virtually all the hardwood-furniture businesses that were once central to the local economy have closed. But in March and April the area comes alive with sugar-making, for Richford stands near the center of Franklin County, the largest syrup-producing area in Vermont.

25.8 In front of the redbrick All Saints Roman Catholic Church, turn left onto VT 105 East.

26.5 Just 0.2 mile beyond Richford Villa Mobile Home Park (on your right), turn right onto South Richford Road.

You immediately start up a tough hill. It rises steeply for about 0.7 mile and then continues gradually but relentlessly for 2.5 miles more to the top. The road then goes wonderfully downhill all the way to Montgomery! And just before you reach the end, you skim across the Fuller or Blackfalls covered bridge, the third local bridge built by Sheldon and Savannah Jewett. It opened in 1890 and crosses Black Falls Creek.

33.7 At the stop sign in Montgomery, turn right onto VT 118 North and ride 25 yards to the Black Lantern Inn (on your left), where you began. Walk across.

Bicycle Repair Services

First Trax, 40 Main Street, Montgomery Center, VT (802-326-3073)

Foot of the Notch Bicycles, VT 108, Jeffersonville, VT (802-644-8182)

Porter's Bike Shop, 116 Grand Avenue, Swanton, VT (802-868-7417)